P9-CKR-626

Epic
MAD®

Also available from MAD Books

Insanely Awesome MAD

Spy vs. Spy Omnibus

MAD About Super Heroes Vol. 2

Spy vs. Spy: The Top Secret Files!

Plus

MAD's Greatest Artists: Sergio Aragonés (Running Press)

The MAD Fold-In Collection 1964-2010 (Chronicle Books)

Spy vs. Spy 2: The Joke and Dagger Files (Watson-Guptill Publications)

MAD About *Star Wars* (Ballantine Books - Del Rey)

MAD Archives Volume 3 (DC Comics)

MAD Kindle Fire eBooks

MAD About Super Heroes Vol. 1

MAD About Super Heroes Vol. 2

MAD About the 50s

MAD About the 60s

MAD About the Oscars

Epic MAD®

By
"The Usual Gang of Idiots"

CONTRIBUTING WRITERS AND ARTISTS:
"The Usual Gang of Idiots"

Published by MAD Books. An imprint of E.C. Publications, Inc., 1700 Broadway, New York, NY 10019.
A Warner Bros. Entertainment Company.

Printed by RR Donnelley, Salem, VA, USA. 3/2/12. First Printing.
ISBN: 978-1-4012-3762-2

Certified Chain of Custody
At Least 25% Certified Forest Content
www.sfiprogram.org
SFI-01042
APPLIES TO TEXT STOCK ONLY

Visit MAD online at: www.madmag.com

CONTENTS

Sergio Aragonés presents a MAD Look

WRITER AND ARTIST: SERGIO ARAGONÉS

at BULLIES

EATS MEETS JEST DEPT.

The MAD WORLD of..

Excuse me, we're wondering what we should order.

Tell the server you want 我希望支付那其它夫婦.

You just ate! You can't swim for an hour or you'll get cramps.
My teacher told me that's a myth that's been disproved.
Listen, just because it's not true doesn't make it all right!
FOOD
WRITER: STAN SINBERG
ARTIST: MARC HEMPEL
Congratulations! How long have you been pregnant?
I'm not...
I'm just eating for two...
I did, thank you. Good night.
Here you go. I'll take that when you're ready.
What? This is a mistake! We didn't order yet!
But you just told me, "I'd like to pay for that other couple."
When my grandchildren were little, they couldn't get enough of my old-world sausage and ham cooking...
When they were teenagers they said, "We can't eat your cooking. It'll make us fat." For years they wouldn't even set foot in my kitchen.
Then the Atkins Diet got hot and fatty food was suddenly in.
Dr. ATKINS' even newer DIET REVOLUTION
I'm BACK, baby!

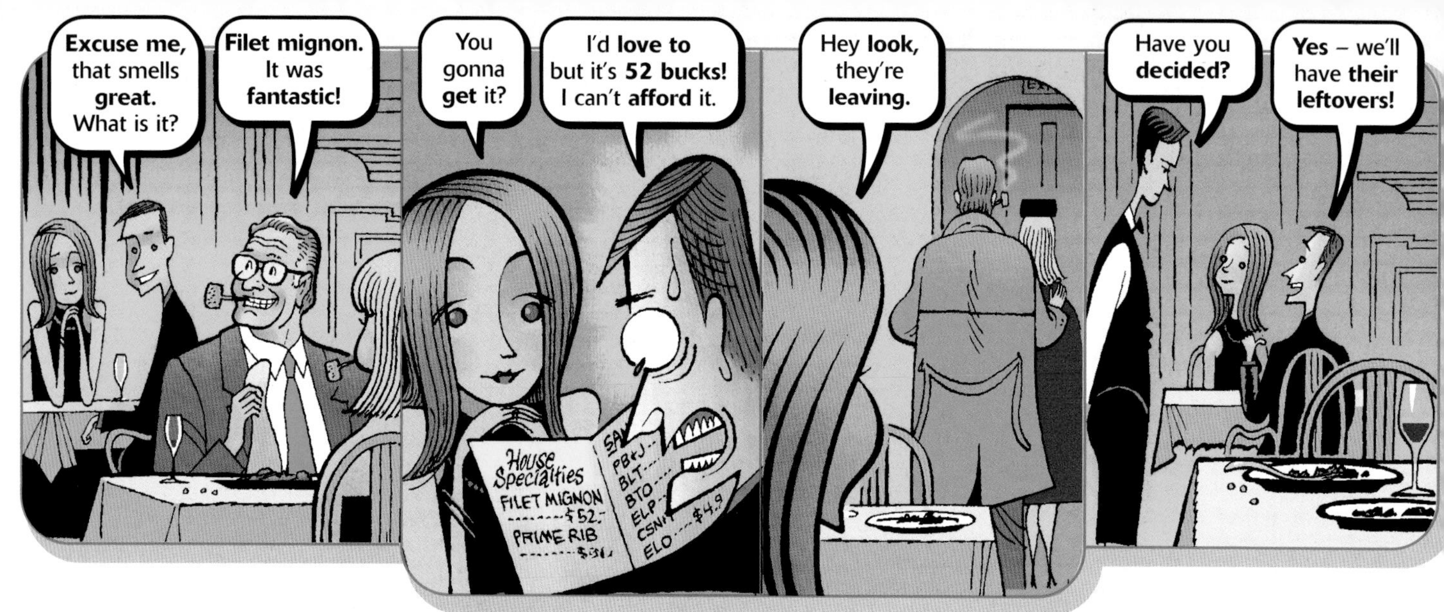

What would you like on your pizza? Sausage? Mushrooms?

The works!

What would you like on your sundae? Whipped cream? Nuts?

The works!

What would you like for your stomach? Antacid? Alka-Seltzer?

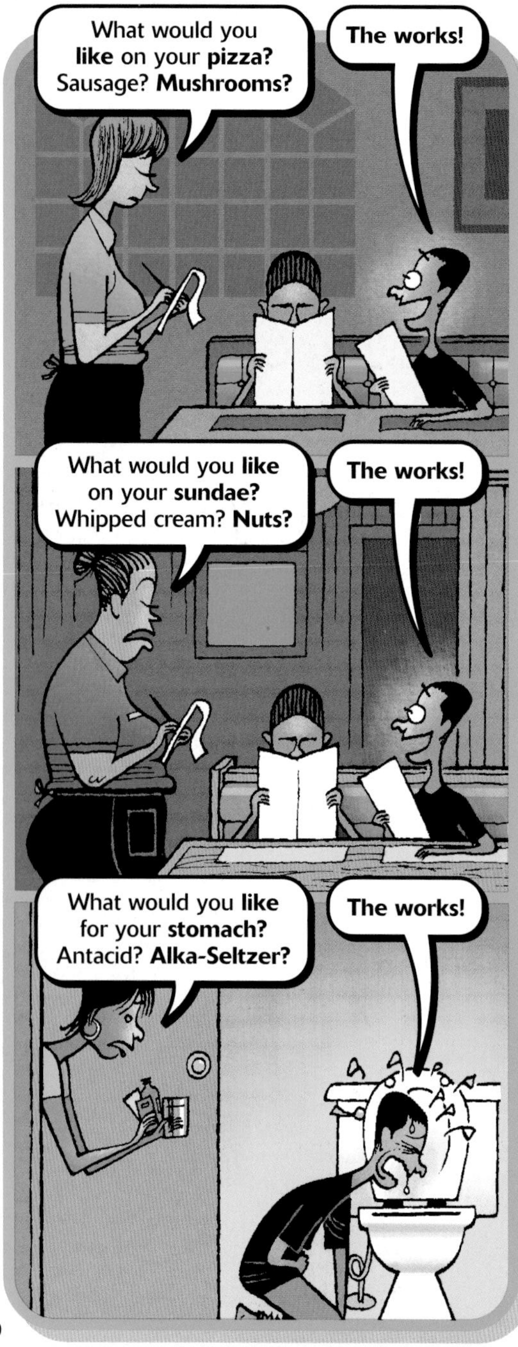

The works!

Today at school, the kids made fun of my eating disorder.

Your WHAT? You don't have an eating disorder. You eat three balanced, nutritious meals a day.

At my school, that IS an eating disorder!

DOG CATCHER

Boy, I am really out of shape. I'd do almost anything to lose weight.

Well, all you have to do is eat less.

I said ALMOST anything!

THE DWAYNE CHRONICLES

WRITER AND ARTIST: ERIC SCOTT

GALACTICKLE DEPT.
IN A GALAXY MILLIONS OF LIGHT YEARS AWAY, A BAD EVIL GALACTIC EMPIRE HAS PLANS FOR A SUPER SPACE STATION THAT CAN DESTROY AN ENTIRE PLANET. LED BY GOOD PRINCESS LAIDUP, REBEL FORCES STEAL THE PLANS...AND A MIGHTY STAR WAR TAKES PLACE
That rotten, evil Galactic Empire . . . killing and destroying everything in sight!!
Wiping out planets and civilization, I can almost excuse. But when they start picking on poor defenseless movie introductions . . .
Hey, clue me in . . . How do we tell the GOOD GUYS from the BAD GUYS around here, anyway?!
Simple! The WHITES are BAD! The BLACKS are GOOD!
Where'd they get that idea from, Ganoomo Sajo . . . the ruler of Mars?
No, Muhammad Ali . . . the ruler of Earth!
If us BAD guys are in WHITE, and the GOOD guys are in BLACK . . . what's our Leader doing dressed in Black . . .?
You may not believe this, but he hasn't changed his costume in 20 years! It started OUT white, but with all his dirty work . . .
You are now in my power, Princess Laidup! Return the plans you stole, and I'll make it worth your while!
You can't bribe me, Zader! You forget, I'm fearless and honest and decent and incor-ruptible!
Come on! Where are the plans?
If you must know, I gave them to a pair of robots!
You gave them to a pair of ROBOTS?!
I never said I was SMART!!
LOCAL MAIL
DOMESTIC MAIL
FOREIGN MAIL

Incredible! Our ship goes faster than the speed of light, and our guns fire almost as fast as the speed of light!
Yeah . . . so guess what just happened! We shot ourselves down!!
What?! You mean to tell me that the In-Flight Movie is Bugs Bunny chasing the Roadrunner up a hill?!?
What do you expect on a seven second flight . . . "The Godfather"?
How high up into space would you say this ship goes?
Quiet! I'm about to say a prayer before we go into battle . . .
OUR FATHER WHO ART BELOW US IN HEAVEN—
That high, huh?
Boy, these space ships are noisy!! Maybe that's why they call this movie . . .
STAR ROARS
ARTIST: HARRY NORTH, ESQ. WRITER: LARRY SIEGEL WITH DICK DE BARTOLO
We got away, Bar-Stool! So far, so good! The Princess depends on us! Our mission must not fail!
Beedeep! Boop! Tweet!
TRANSLATION: If we're both robots, Cree-Pio, how come we look—and talk—so different?
Because I happen to be a magnificent, articulate golden Adonis, and you're a sawed-off, incoherent, stupid sack of bolts!
Beedeep! Boop!
TRANSLATION: I knew there had to be a scientific reason for it!
ESCAP CAPSU C
Goodness gracious, this planet simply screams for some—Je ne sais quoi—in the way of decor! Still, in some ways, it's a veritable Shangri-La! Take my hand, Bar-Stool . . . I'm a stranger in paradise . . .
Beedeep! Tweet!
TRANSLATION: As if I don't have enough problems, now I'm stuck with a gay robot!
Bar-Stool, we seem to be lost! Oh, dear . . . look what's coming! Fiendish creatures about to tear us limb from limb and commit unspeakable acts of cruelty upon us . . .!
Follow the yellow sand road! Follow the yellow sand road! Follow . . . follow . . . follow . . . follow . . . Follow the yellow sand road!
Beep! Zit! Gack!
TRANSLATION: And then again . . . there's an outside chance they may be Space Munchkins!
Hi, strangers! I'm Lube Skystalker! I'm a senior at Buffooin Tech, where I major in Incredible Space Heroics!
Gracious, there couldn't be any money in THAT field!
You're telling me! That's why I'm minoring in Space Accounting! Hey, anyone ever tell you you look like an "Oscar"?!?
Take a good look! With your performance in this film, it's as close as you'll ever get to an Academy Award!

We need help! It's our Princess! She's in terrible trouble! I'm now going to press a button on my companion here, and an image will appear with a message that may mean life or death for the entire universe! Here goes . . .
Welcome to "Hollywood Squares"!
Whoops! Wrong button! Don't tell me you get THAT thing up here too!
Yep! There's no way you can keep it out!

Ah, here's the Princess now!
Save me, Oldie Von Moldie . . . wherever you are! You are my only hope! Otherwise, millions of people will be wiped out in a holocaust, the likes of which civilization has never seen!
Is that her whole bit? Just that?
No, actually she closes with a saxophone solo that'll blow your mind! But you get the idea! Lube, you must help us find Oldie Von Moldie!
Hop in my space car!

Look! There's Oldie Von Moldie!! Many years ago, my Father and he were Military Pilots together! Now, he's 97 . . . he can hardly see . . . and his hands shake terribly!
What does he do now?
What else? He's a Commercial Airlines Pilot!

Oldie, Princess Laidup is in the hands of that rat, Zader! We haven't a moment to lose!
Eh? What's that? You say you want to go up to my flat later and sing the blues??
He doesn't seem to HEAR too well, either!
In his spare time, he moonlights as a Telephone Operator!

Very well, Lube! We will go into town, find us a space ship and rescue Princess Laidup!
But first, I must teach you about the Force . . .
The Force? what's that?!?
It is a Power that is all around us! It is everywhere at all times! It knows all and sees all! It is eternal!
They have something like that on Earth! It's called "The Internal Revenue Service"!

Hold it! Let me see your I.D.!
He doesn't have to show you his I.D.!
He doesn't have to show me his I.D.!
He can go about his business!
He can go about his business!
Gee, Oldie, how did you do that?
The Force gives you power over weak minds!
The Force gives me power over weak minds!
All right! Drive on!
All right! Drive on!

I can lick any mutant in the joint!
I can't go home, Zfrx! My gargoyle doesn't understand me!
Who in heck are you?
Does the name Quasimodo ring a bell?
Funny! This is what I usually see in a bar AFTER I've had a few drinks!
What's so special about this place? It looks like any Singles Bar in any big city on Earth!
I've had too much to drink! I'm seeing weird things!
This bar is FULL of weird things!!
I'm talking about those human forms that just came in! Man, those are WEIRD THINGS!!

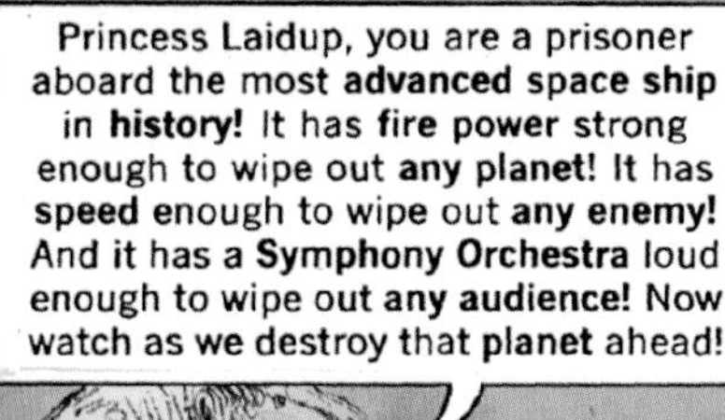

Princess Laidup, you are a prisoner aboard the most **advanced space ship** in **history!** It has **fire power** strong enough to wipe out **any planet!** It has **speed** enough to wipe out **any enemy!** And it has a **Symphony Orchestra** loud enough to wipe out **any audience!** Now watch as we destroy that **planet** ahead!
Excuse me, but I'm from the **Electric Company . . .** and **before** you wipe out any more planets, you'll have to pay your **bill!** You owe us **$4 million** in **back payments,** and **that's** just for **YESTERDAY!!**
BILL
FINAL DEMAND
FOR WASTING
RIGA IV.....
...$4,000,000

I suddenly feel a **sick sensation** in my stomach . . . like a million souls crying out in terror! It's . . . an **incredible disturbance,** I feel . . .
Perhaps the Death Ship has blown up an **entire planet . . . ?**
Perhaps . . . ! Then again, it might be the radishes I had for lunch . . . !

Look! It's the evil Galactic Empire **Death Ship Space Station . . .** straight ahead of us!
Let's get out of here!
We **can't!** We've **lost control!** We're being **drawn toward it!** They have their X-5-G Nuclear Hoover-Matic on **"Full Suck"!!**

I've got **good** news and **bad** news! First, the **bad news!** That Death Ship **Space Port** is jammed with **50,000 heavily armed bad guys!**
Gulp! What's the **GOOD NEWS?**
We probably **won't** have to go through **Baggage Claim!!**

Remember, lads, try to act **nonchalant!**
Anybody come by your **post,** Zargg?
Yeah! A party of **six!** Two guys, a 97-year-old man, a couple of robots, and a 14-foot ape!
Okay . . . but if you see any-thing **UNUSUAL,** let me know!

Here's my **first plan,** men! **You** fellows . . . take over the **Control Room** and rescue the **Princess . . .** and **I'll** take care of **Zader!!**
Look, Oldie! The bad guys have **spotted** us!
Okay . . . here's my **second plan . . . RUN LIKE HELL!!**

Your Highness, I'm Lube Skystalker! I'm majoring in "Incredible Space Heroics" at Buffooin Tech! As my Term Project, I decided to organize an army, find a convenient space ship, rescue you, and fly you six billion miles to safety on the planet, Draidel!
Don't even mention it! God . . . who wants to be a Space Accountant!
This is madness! You know what happens if you fail?!
PLEASE KNOCK AND ENTER

And what is your reason for doing it, Mr. Yoyo . . . ?
Princess, I'm doing it for the money!!
Then I will see to it that you get plenty! I will give you $20 million!
Wow! Just think of what I can buy with $20 million!
Well, if you go to Earth, you can buy a tank of gas for $20 million! This is 2012, you know...!
BEWARE OF DOG

What fantastic luck! Who arranged for you to carry a handy rope on your belt with a hook that happens to fit over that projection so we can swing over this bottomless pit?
Probably the same clever guy who saw to it that 500 sharpshooters could fire at us and miss from a distance of ten feet!

What's happening? Where are we? The walls are starting to close in!!
Great!! We're not only in the world's largest Space Station . . . we're also in the world's largest Trash Compactor!
Well, at least they won't find us here!
And if they DO find us, they won't recognize us! They'll be looking for FULL-SIZED people!!

So, Zader! We meet again! Prepare your Light Ray Sword for a duel to the death! I shall triumph because I have The Force!
Get ready to die, you black-hearted villain!!
Good lord! My light ray has gone out!!
How ironic! Betrayed by a lack of faith in The Force . . .
. . . and a ridiculously short . . . gasp . . . extension cord!

Well . . . you **did** it! You **rescued me**, you beat up on the **bad guys**, and now you are about to receive a **hero's welcome** here on **Draidel**!
Hello, people of Draidel . . . !

Terrible news, your Highness! **Zader** is **boiling mad,** and now he's about to **destroy the whole universe!** We need a **courageous pilot** to **save** us!
Lube, I have a **favor** to ask you . . .
Goodbye, people of Draidel!

The enemy is breaking through our **defenses,** Sir! They're using **small one-man ships!** We **never planned** on being **attacked** by anything **that small!**
I **can't believe it!** We build the most **advanced space ship in history,** and nobody thought about putting **SCREENS** on the **windows!?!**

Remember, I am **with** you, Lube!
I **know that,** Oldie!
Do you feel my **presence!**
More than **that,** I feel your **weight!**
So will you **please get off my space ship!** It's only built for **one . . .** and you're going to make me **crash!**
Besides, time is **running out!** We must **penetrate** their **defenses,** enter the **target shaft,** and fire on the **exact spot** that will start a **chain reaction!**
But how will you **know** where that exact spot **is?**
It's a **one** in a **billion** chance!!

Wait a minute . . . !! That may JUST be it!!
THIS WAY
TO DESTROY EVIL GALACTIC EMPIRE
HERE

KER-
BOOM
TINKLE TINKLE

. . . and so, in closing, people of Draidel, I would just like to say that **tyranny** has at long last been **wiped from the face of the universe,** and peace is here! The star wars are **over forever!**
But . . . that's **terrible!** That's simply **awful!!**

Now that we've made the universe **safe,** we've opened it up for the **tourists!!**
WA-AL!
SA-AY!
WHERE CAN I GET A DECENT FRANK
EAT YOUR HEART OUT DISNEY PLANET!
GEE
...LOUSY BEDS!
MOM, I WANNA THROW U—
Y'MEAN THE BROAD'S A REAL PRINCESS?!
BURP

Fairy Tale
SCENES WE'D LIKE TO SEE
THE FROG PRINCE

WRITER AND ARTIST: DON MARTIN

ROMAN EMPEROR JULIUS SNEEZER

FILMMAKER GEORGE MUCUS

INDIAN PRINCESS PICK-AHONTAS

PRESIDENT TEDDY NOSE-EVEL

To create a masterpiece, you must **dig deep**!

PAINTER PABLO PICK-CASSO

Ewww is equal to a **Massive Chunk**, squared!

$E=mc^2$

SCIENTIST ALBERT EIN-SLIME

SINGER ICK JAGGER

EXPLORER CRUST-OPHER COLUMBUS

Planet TAD!!!!!

http://www.galaxyo'blogs.com/planettad

Search

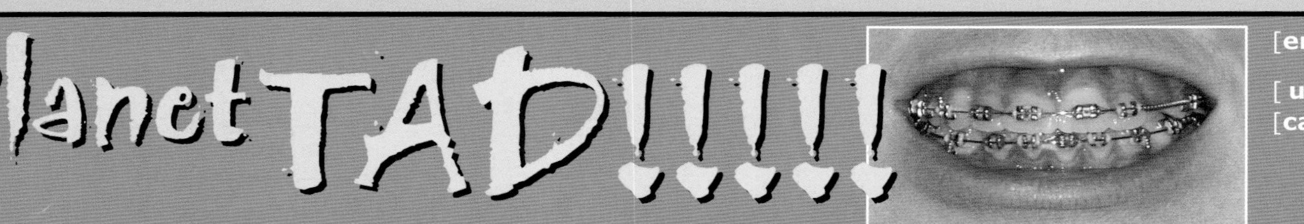

[**entries**|archive|friends]

[**userinfo**|galaxyo'blogs userinfo]
[**calendar**|galaxyo'blogs calendar]

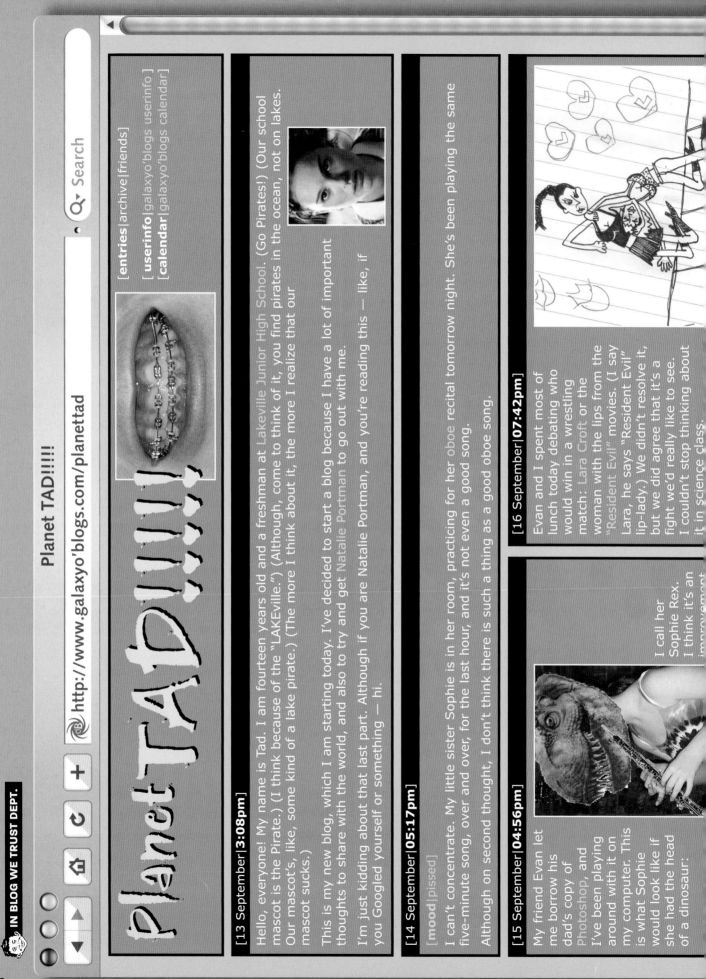

[13 September|**3:08pm**]

Hello, everyone! My name is Tad. I am fourteen years old and a freshman at Lakeville Junior High School. (Go Pirates!) (Our school mascot is the Pirate.) (I think because of the "LAKEville.") (Although, come to think of it, you find pirates in the ocean, not on lakes. Our mascot's, like, some kind of a lake pirate.) (The more I think about it, the more I realize that our mascot sucks.)

This is my new blog, which I am starting today. I've decided to start a blog because I have a lot of important thoughts to share with the world, and also to try and get Natalie Portman to go out with me.

I'm just kidding about that last part. Although if you are Natalie Portman, and you're reading this — like, if you Googled yourself or something — hi.

[14 September|**05:17pm**]

[**mood**|pissed]

I can't concentrate. My little sister Sophie is in her room, practicing for her oboe recital tomorrow night. She's been playing the same five-minute song, over and over, for the last hour, and it's not even a good song.

Although on second thought, I don't think there is such a thing as a good oboe song.

[15 September|**04:56pm**]

My friend Evan let me borrow his dad's copy of Photoshop, and I've been playing around with it on my computer. This is what Sophie would look like if she had the head of a dinosaur:

I call her Sophie Rex. I think it's an

[16 September|**07:42pm**]

Evan and I spent most of lunch today debating who would win in a wrestling match: Lara Croft or the woman with the lips from the "Resident Evil" movies. (I say Lara, he says "Resident Evil" lip-lady.) We didn't resolve it, but we did agree that it's a fight we'd really like to see. I couldn't stop thinking about it in science class.

[17 September|11:22am]

I saw a preview of King Kong on TV last night. I think if I were a giant ape trying to escape from people in airplanes trying to kill me, maybe I wouldn't climb to the top of the city's highest skyscraper. Duh!

[19 September|03:01pm]

[**mood**|pissed]

I can't stand Doug Spivak. He tried tripping me today. He calls me "Tard," which I guess is a play on my name. It would hurt my feelings that he's making fun of my intelligence, but Doug's the guy who read half of "Watership Down" for English class before he realized it was about rabbits.

[20 September|03:19pm]

[**mood**|pissed]

Bad news. Mom found a printout of Sophie Rex. She and Dad say I'm not allowed to use Photoshop on pictures of Sophie anymore. But she didn't say anything about pictures of THEM.

This is what my parents looked like when they were newly married, and if they had chipmunk heads.

[21 September|05:31pm]

In English today, Mr. Carlson had us spend the whole class diagramming sentences at the blackboard. Diagramming sentences is like a combination of the worst parts of doing math with the worst parts of doing English. It's a total waste of time, because you can either speak English or you can't, and if you can't there's no point in drawing lines all over your sentences. Doug Spivak thinks that "gooder" means the same thing as "better" and no amount of diagramming sentences will fix that.

Besides, it's a waste of time. I asked Dad at dinner whether there's any job where you have to diagram sentences, and he said, "Teaching junior high kids English."

Mr. Carlson hard at work.

[22 September|07:47pm]

Today Mr. Carlson had us diagram sentences again. I told him that I didn't want to have to keep doing this, because the only job where you have to diagram sentences is junior high teacher, and I planned on doing something better than that. He didn't say anything, he just got very quiet and gave us all a pop quiz on diagramming sentences. I got a D. Doug Spivak blamed me for the pop quiz, and he told me to meet him behind the gym after school so he could kick my butt. I decided not to go.

WRITER: TIM CARVELL ARTIST: BRIAN DURNIAK

JOKE AND DAGGER DEPT.

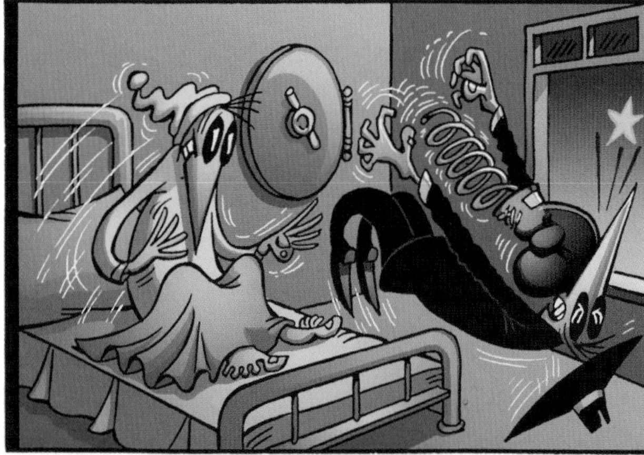

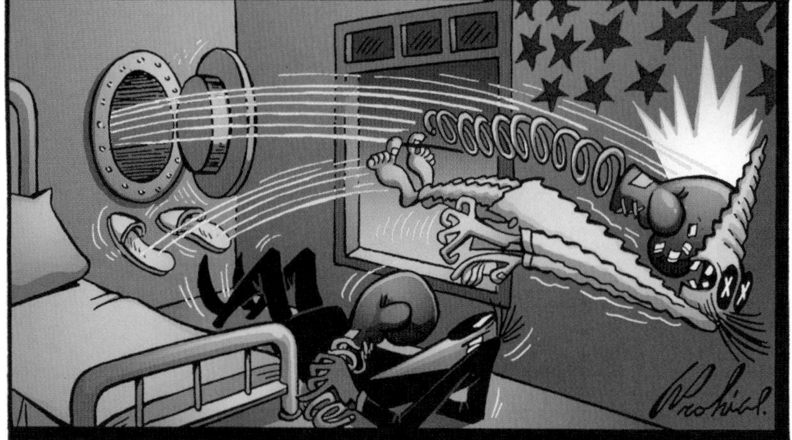

WRITER AND ARTIST: ANTONIO PROHIAS COLORIST: CARRIE STRACHAN

IF LEMONY SNICKET WROTE ABOUT THE SERIES OF UNFORTUNATE EVENTS IN YOUR LIFE

Your Series of Unfortunate Events
HELP
SCHOOL BUS
KEEP BACK 50 FEET
Book the Dth
by LEMONY SNICKET
THE DEMENTED DRIVER

ARTIST: GARY HALLGREN

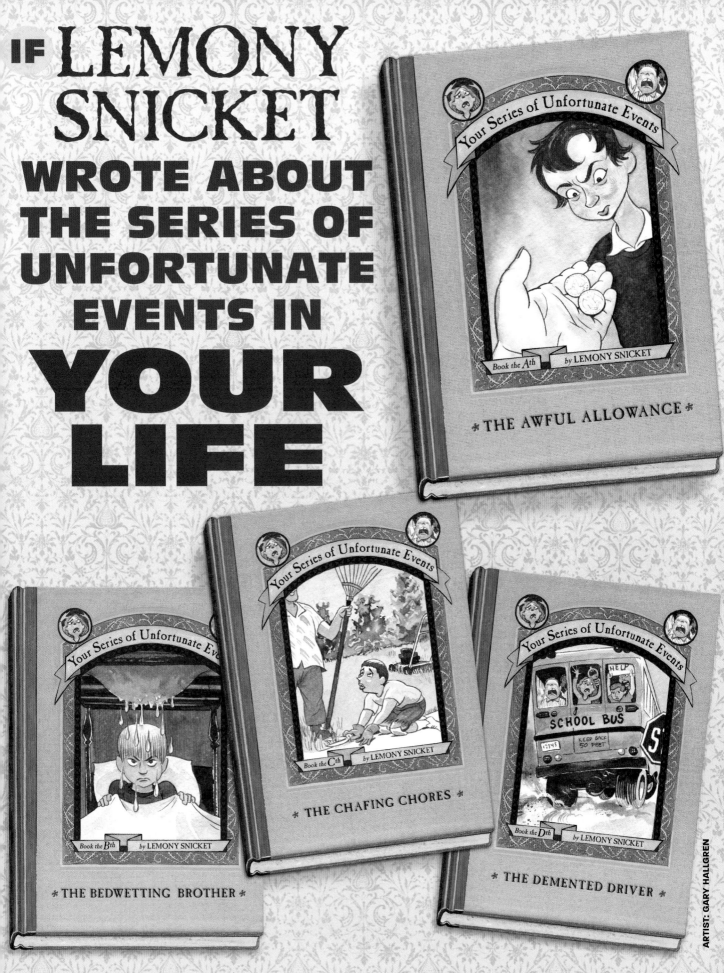

Your Series of Unfortunate Events
Book the Eth
by LEMONY SNICKET
THE EVIL EGGING
Your Series of Unfortunate Events
Book the Fth
by LEMONY SNICKET
THE FATAL FISHTANK
Your Series of Unfortunate Events
Book the Gth
by LEMONY SNICKET
THE GASSY GRANDPARENTS
SOLVE BY MON.
READ 140 PP IN GEO TEXT.
DO ALL 50 PROBLEMS
Book the Hth
by LEMONY SNICKET
THE HORRIFIC HOMEWORK
Your Series of Unfortunate Events
Book the Ith
by LEMONY SNICKET
THE INESCAPABLE IMMUNIZATION
Your Series of Unfortunate Events
Book the Jth
by LEMONY SNICKET
THE JUVENILE JAMMIES
Your Series of Unfortunate Events
Book the Kth
by LEMONY SNICKET
THE KILLER KARATE CLASS
Your Series of Unfortunate Events
Book the Lth
by LEMONY SNICKET
THE LOUSY LUNCH

Your Series of Unfortunate Events
Book the Mth
by LEMONY SNICKET
THE MEDDLING MOTHER
Your Series of Unfortunate Events
Book the Nth
by LEMONY SNICKET
THE NASTY NECKTIE
Your Series of Unfortunate Events
Book the Oth
by LEMONY SNICKET
THE OBNOXIOUS ORNAMENT
Your Series of Unfortunate Events
Book the Pth
by LEMONY SNICKET
THE PATHETIC PAGEANT
Your Series of Unfortunate Events
Huge test
Book the Qth
by LEMONY SNICKET
THE QUEASY QUIZ
Your Series of Unfortunate Events
Book the Rth
by LEMONY SNICKET
THE RAINY RECESS
Your Series of Unfortunate Events
Book the Sth
by LEMONY SNICKET
THE SWELTERING SUMMER SCHOOL
Your Series of Unfortunate Events
Book the Tth
by LEMONY SNICKET
THE TORTUOUS TRIP

THE UNFASHIONABLE UNIFORM

THE VILE VEGETABLES

THE WICKED WEDGIE

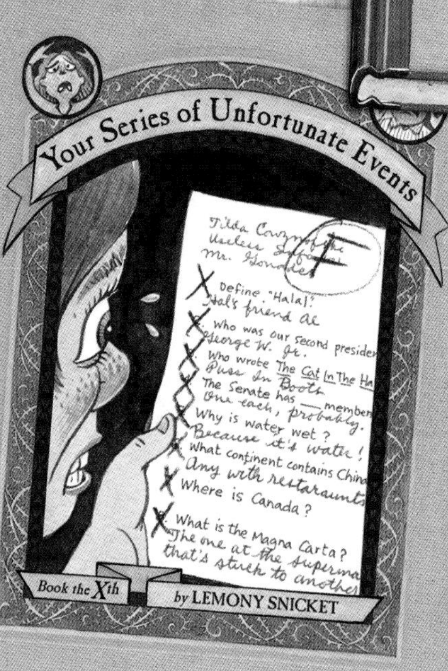

THE EXCESSIVE X'S

THE YUCKY YARD SALE

Your Series of Unfortunate Events
ZIPPP
Book the Zth
by LEMONY SNICKET

THE ZEALOUS ZIPPERER

ANOTHER MORNING ON FIFTH AVENUE

ARTIST: PAUL COKER WRITER: DUCK EDWING

SONGS for PEOPLE

(ALL SONGS MAY BE SUNG TO THE TUNE OF THE SPONGEBOB SQUAREPANTS THEME!)

THE LUNCH LADY

Who's dishing up food that's
disgustingly gross?
The Lunch Lady!
Is anything edible? Not even close!
The Lunch Lady!

If you're feeling brave give
the chili a try!
The Lunch Lady!
That is if you think
it's your day to die!

Ready!

Her big lunch treat!
Is some brown meat!
Smells like bad feet!
We say – don't eat!

OUR MATH TEACHER

Whose class is so boring it puts us to sleep?
Our Math Teacher!
Gives homework so tough that we go home and weep
Our Math Teacher!

He dreams about fractions, thinks angles are neat,
Our Math Teacher!
Likes to convert things from inches to feet!
Our Math Teacher!

Ready!

We hate his class!
It's like bad gas!
He's a jackass!
No way – we'll pass!

in YOUR SCHOOL

THE CLASS BULLY

Who's big and who's scary and
mean as can be?
The Class Bully!
He beats you up daily at twenty to three!
The Class Bully!

When you see him coming it's
best just to run!
The Class Bully!
A wedgie for you is his kind of fun!

Ready!

All brawn, no brain!
Loves to give pain!
He can't refrain!
He's just – insane!

WRITER: ANDREW J. SCHWARTZBERG ARTIST: TOM RICHMOND

SCHOOL BUS DRIVER

Who drives on the sidewalk and
blows through red lights?
School Bus Driver!
His hearing is going and his vision bites!
School Bus Driver!

We wonder how he got his license at all!
School Bus Driver!
We think it's a fake he bought at the mall!

Ready!

Our bones will break!
In fear we quake!
Please sir, please brake!
A cab – we'll take!

WORDS TO GLIB BY DEPT.

Parents, teachers and other authority figures have a miraculous gift fo shutting off any topic of conversation they don't wish to pursue. They just come out of left field with some obscure, presumably wise old saying

MAD PROVERBS GUARANTEED

WRITER: TOM KOC

r axiom which you don't understand. But now you can have the power to ilence THEIR boring, insipid and unwanted talk, simply by memorizing this ifty collection of deeply philosophical, but absolutely meaningless...

TO LEAVE 'EM SPEECHLESS

RTIST: AL JAFFEE

A PROVERB IN THE HAND IS WORTH TWO IN THE MOUTH

You can't ride a wet horse to Germany!

Only a fool leaves his laundry with a red-headed woman!

You can't tell a Canadian by the color of his underwear!

There is more kindness in one smile than in five pounds of beef liver!

Never accuse a pygmy of being short until you have walked a mile in his moccasins!

If you scratch a Conservative, does he not stop itching?

Merely hoping the world is flat won't help you fall off it!

No one will ever know you've dug a hole if you leave the dirt in it!

If it can't be done, stop doing it!

A good woman is like a stucco bird cage—rough on the outside, but heavy!

Why trade damp firewood for the love of a bearded butcher?

Life is like a can of pears, only more oblong!

If a chicken is happy in the barnyard, why teach it to sell real estate?

DON MARTIN DEPT.

ONE FINE DAY DURING LUNCH PERIOD

WRITER AND ARTIST: DON MARTIN

Cents-Less Coupons

OUR MONEY-SAVING CIRCULAR

DENTA-FROST

Toothpaste & Cake Frosting

NEW!

So Sweet it Hurts Your Teeth—While CLEANING Them!*

*Clinically proven to fight cavities while causing them. (ADA Report, 3/2002)

TRY ALL FIVE ANTISEPTIC VARIETIES!

NEW! DENTA-FROST
Toothpaste & Cake Frosting
Flaque-Fighting Coconut Pecan
NET WT. 12 OZ (340g)

A MAD FAKEOUT AD

NEW!
DENTA-FROST
Toothpaste & Cake Frosting
Chocolate Fudge with Whitening Power™
NET WT. 12 OZ (340g)

NEW!
DENTA-FROST
Toothpaste & Cake Frosting
Tartar-Control Cream Cheese Supreme™
NET WT. 12 OZ (340g)

NEW!
DENTA-FROST
Toothpaste & Cake Frosting
Sparkling Milk Chocolate
NET WT. 12 OZ (340g)

MANUFACTURER'S COUPON
NOT VALID IN AMERICA

SAVE 25¢

when you buy any flavor
DENTA-FROST
Toothpaste & Cake Frosting

Consumer: If you try to use this coupon in a supermarket, the cashier will not only start laughing and pointing, but will call over the other cashiers, who will also start laughing and pointing, and all the shoppers waiting on line will get angry at you. It's true!

Somedays you just don't have time to shoot, fetch and skin a mess of squirrels for vittles.

And who can afford fresh squirrel at supermarket prices? Inbred Valley to the rescue!

SKWIRL™ Imitation Squirrel Meat tastes just like the real thing. Affordable, too! And we reckon that furry little guy in the oak tree just might thank you.

MANUFACTURER'S COUPON
EXPIRES APRIL 30, 1971

Save 75¢

When you purchase ONE 6 ounce package of Inbred Valley SKWIRL™ Imitation Squirrel Meat

Consumer: Lose weight now, ask me how! I lost 40 pounds in 2 months! You can too! No dieting, exercise, etc. Call 800-555-5728 for details. 24 hr. recorded message.

SKWIRL™

Qwik & Easy Skwirl™-Loaf

1 package (6 oz.) SKWIRL™ Imitation Squirrel Meat
1 cup catsup
2 handfuls bread, mooshed-up*

1. Dump all 'gredients in a pot.
2. Scrunch into a loafy shape.
3. Put in oven.
4. Bake until cooked.

Serves 2 to 14 pendin' on how many mouths need feedin'.

*sawdust may be substituted

"I used to have to threaten to put the cat to sleep before the kids would clean the litter box. Now they can't wait to do it!"

NEW!

FUNCLUMPS™

SHAPE-CLUMPING CAT LITTER

Eliminates Odor!
Reduces Tracking!
Clumps Urine Into Fun Shapes!

MFR COUPON EXPIRES NOW

FUNCLUMPS™

$1 OFF

Shape-Clumping Cat Litter

Consumer: Call us up and let us know when and where you're going to try and use this coupon. We want to see you explain to the store manager why you're trying to redeem a coupon for a product that does not exist. On second thought, don't call us. We know how you'll sound: very, very stupid!

A MAD FAKEOUT AD

SERGIO ARAGONÉS Presents a MAD look

at PAINTBALL

PAINT BALL

FLAG

SPLATT!

PAINT BALL

URBAN QUEST
PAINTBALL PLAYING FIELD
OXNARD CA
BARREL PLUGS IN

GRRR!

SPLAT!

ART
GALLERY

G*!!*@!
Grrr
OJAI SURPLUS

SPLATT!
SPLATT!

SPLAT!

G*!!*

? ?

SPLATT!

THAWP! THAWP!
THAP! THAP!

ARAGONÉS

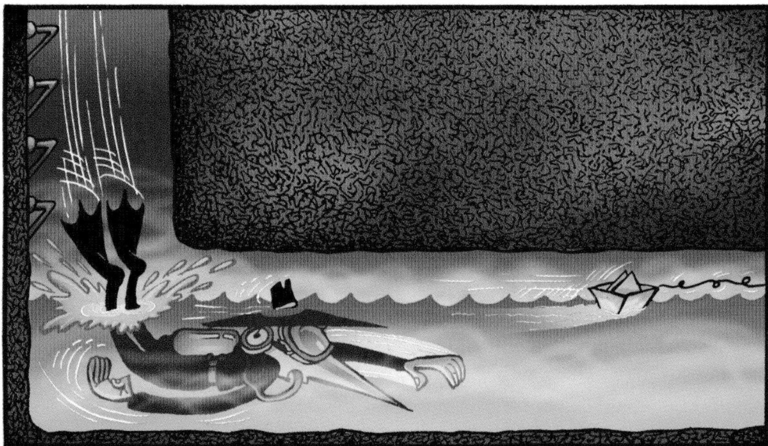

WRITER AND ARTIST: ANTONIO PROHIAS COLORIST: CARRIE STRACHAN

Is it just us or are the standards for qualifying as human just a tad lower at game rooms? You look around and what do you see? Geeks, dweebs and pinheads walking from game to game with a fistful of quarters pretending they have a life! Yes, and every one of these pathetic losers has their place in MAD's gallery of...

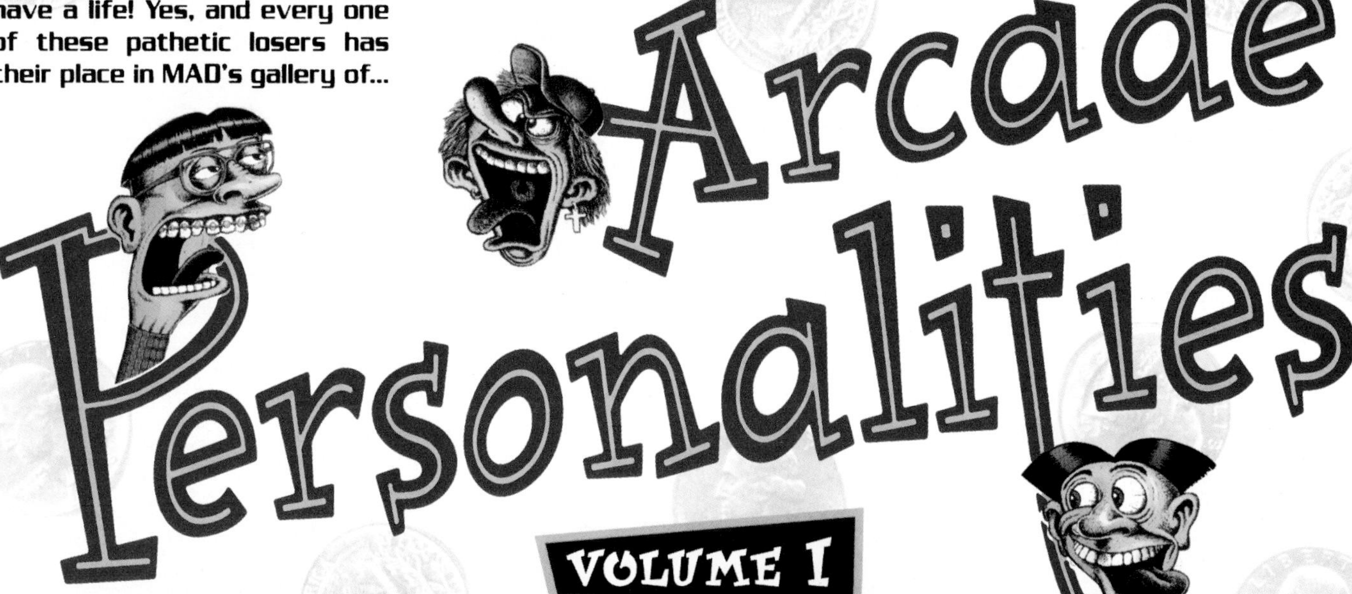

Video Arcade Personalities

VOLUME I

WRITER: SEAN EISENPORTH
ARTIST: TOM BUNK

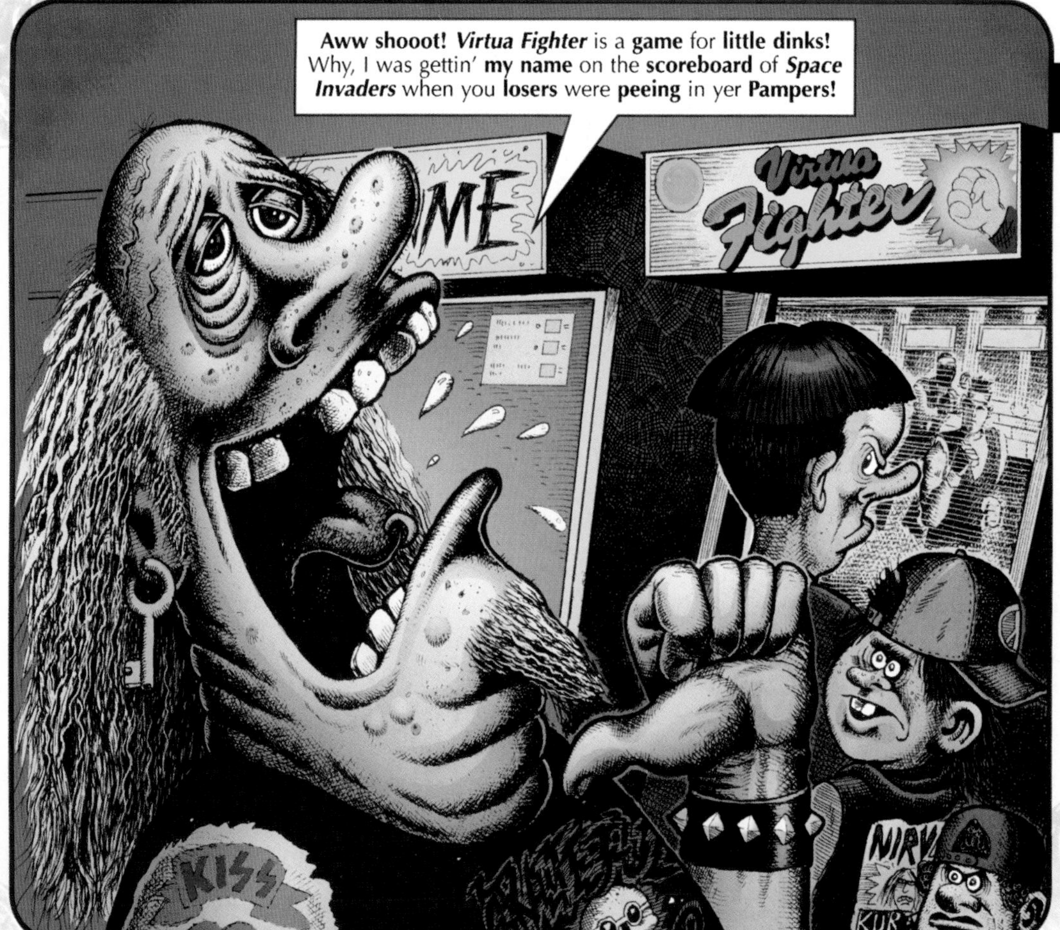

Aww shoooot! *Virtua Fighter* is a game for little dinks! Why, I was gettin' my name on the scoreboard of *Space Invaders* when you losers were peeing in yer Pampers!
ME
Virtua Fighter
KISS

THE VETERAN

Yeah yeah, The Veteran may have been a big shooter back in the ancient times of *Space Invaders* and *Asteroids*, but those days are long gone. Even so, that doesn't stop this legendary-blowhard/has-been from clinging desperately to his past and blabbering on about how cool he was back in 1981. Memo to The Veteran: No one gives a rat's butt!

Video Arcade Personalities

MR. NO-FRIENDS

Sure, you have to feel sorry for the guy, but whatever you do, don't make eye contact with Mr. No-Friends! If he starts yakking at you anyway, the best course of action is to just pretend you're deaf, because if you acknowledge him even once, he will stick to you like HERPES!

Yeah, so then I **found out** there's a **secret passage** on **Level 3** that lets you **WARP** directly into the **ZAP Dimension!** Like, it **should have** been **obvious,** right? But it **wasn't!** Hey, do **you** read ***Gamepro?*** I read ***Gamepro!*** I guess you can **tell, huh?**
DIE HARD
GAME PRO
TOKENS 25¢ OR 3 for $ 1.00

THE GAME HOG

Not even a lengthy line-up of pissed-off homeboys can deter The Game Hog from monopolizing the hot, new game at the arcade. He continues to feed an endless supply of quarters into the slot, blissfully unaware of the hostility brewing behind his back. This explains why many Game Hogs never live to see their 21st birthday!

THE SUPER DADDY

He loves his kids — so much, in fact, that he takes them everywhere — even to the arcade! The Super Daddy does this because he's deeply committed to his child's personal growth and emotional development. That's why he sticks Junior between two video games for several hours — because it builds character!!

THE SCAVENGER

This pathetic loser carefully and systematically checks each and every machine coin return slot in a desperate search for unclaimed quarters. His ultimate gratification comes, however, when he finds a scoreboard where someone hasn't inserted their name. The Scavenger, of course, still lives at home with his parents!

COMING SOON...VOLUME II!

Good news! Zombies are making a comeback! It used to be that these creatures were feared and despised by the general population, but no more! Still, don't pop those champagne corks for zombies just yet! Being a zombie ain't easy, as you'll see in...

JOHN CALDWELL'S

THINGS THAT REALLY GET UNDER A ZOMBIE'S SKIN

WRITER AND ARTIST: JOHN CALDWELL

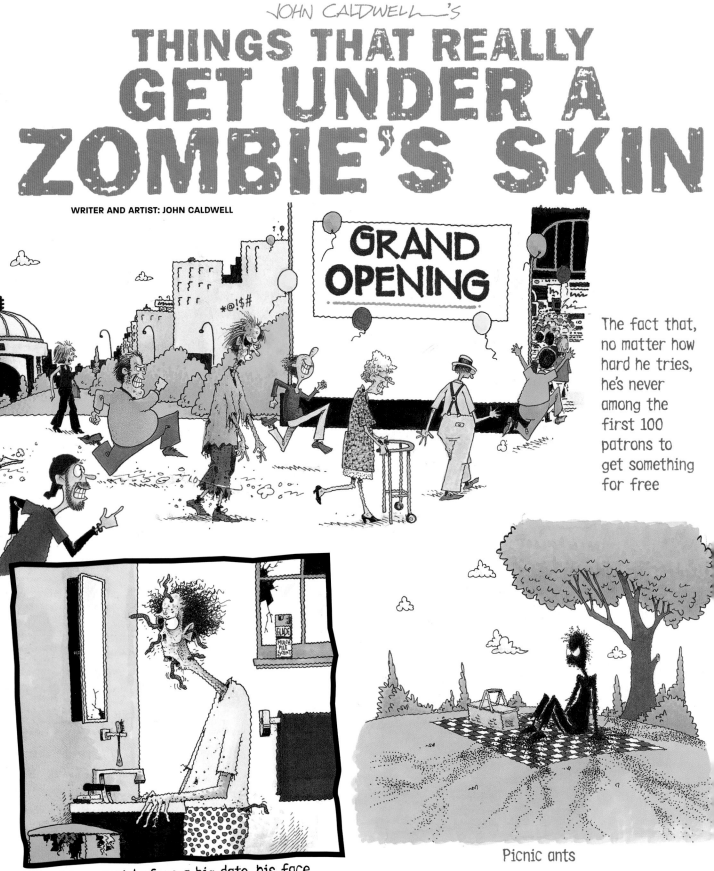

The fact that, no matter how hard he tries, he's never among the first 100 patrons to get something for free

When, just before a big date, his face breaks out in nightcrawlers

Picnic ants

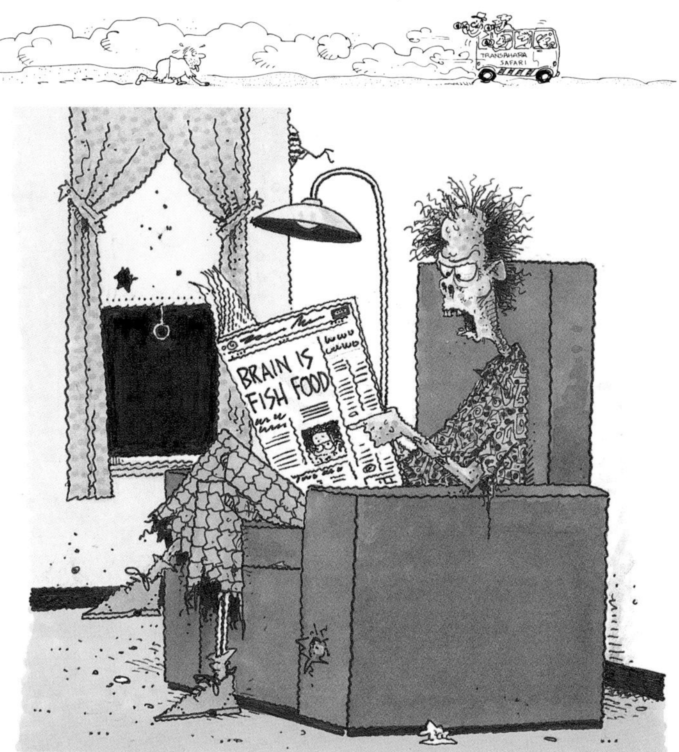

Flip-flopping government studies saying one day that eating brains lowers cholesterol, then the next day, declaring just the opposite

The seemingly insurmountable problems associated with getting a barbed wire bicep tattoo

The time it takes to find a limb that fell off while you were sleeping

Getting Punk'd

Seriously mis-timing that hand-popping-out-from-the-grave moment

THINGS YOU CAN DO FOR YOUR DOG ON HIS BIRTHDAY

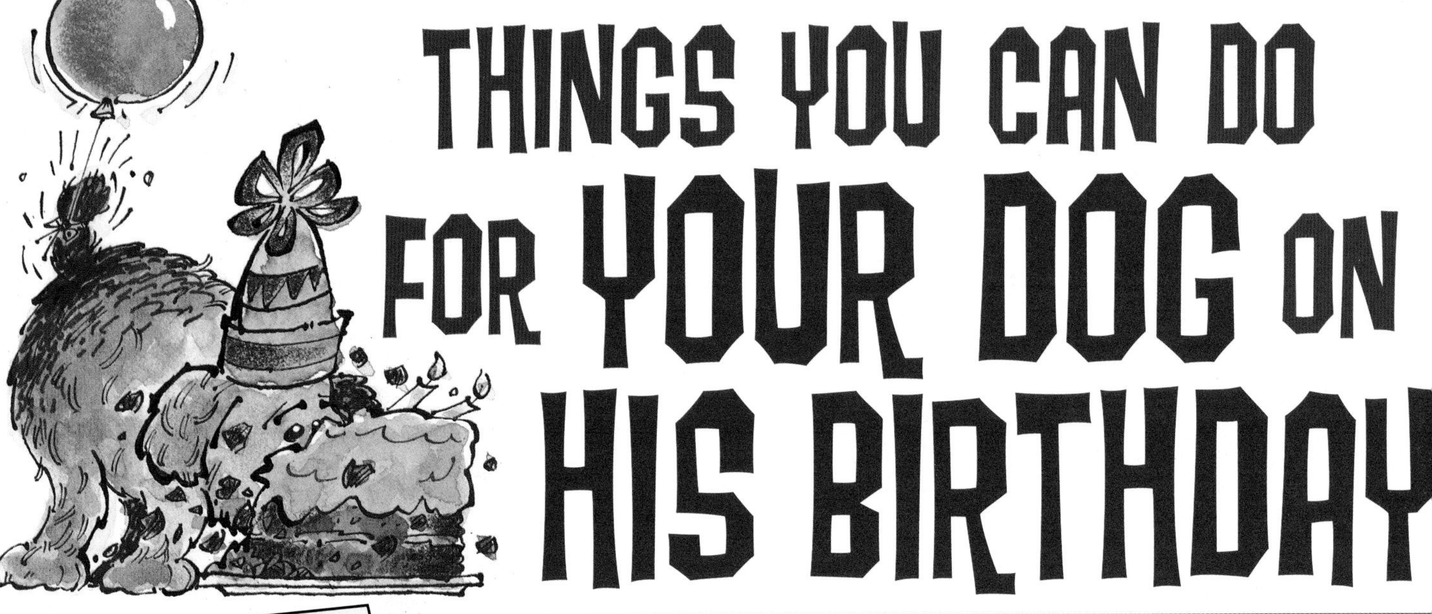

Let him throw his very own party!

Perform a trick for him!

Play "Happy Birthday" on a high-pitched dog whistle!

Share his hobby with him!

Help him dig holes in your neighbor's lawn!

Let him eat first and you get HIS table scraps!

Give him the use of your bed for the day!
Jayhawk

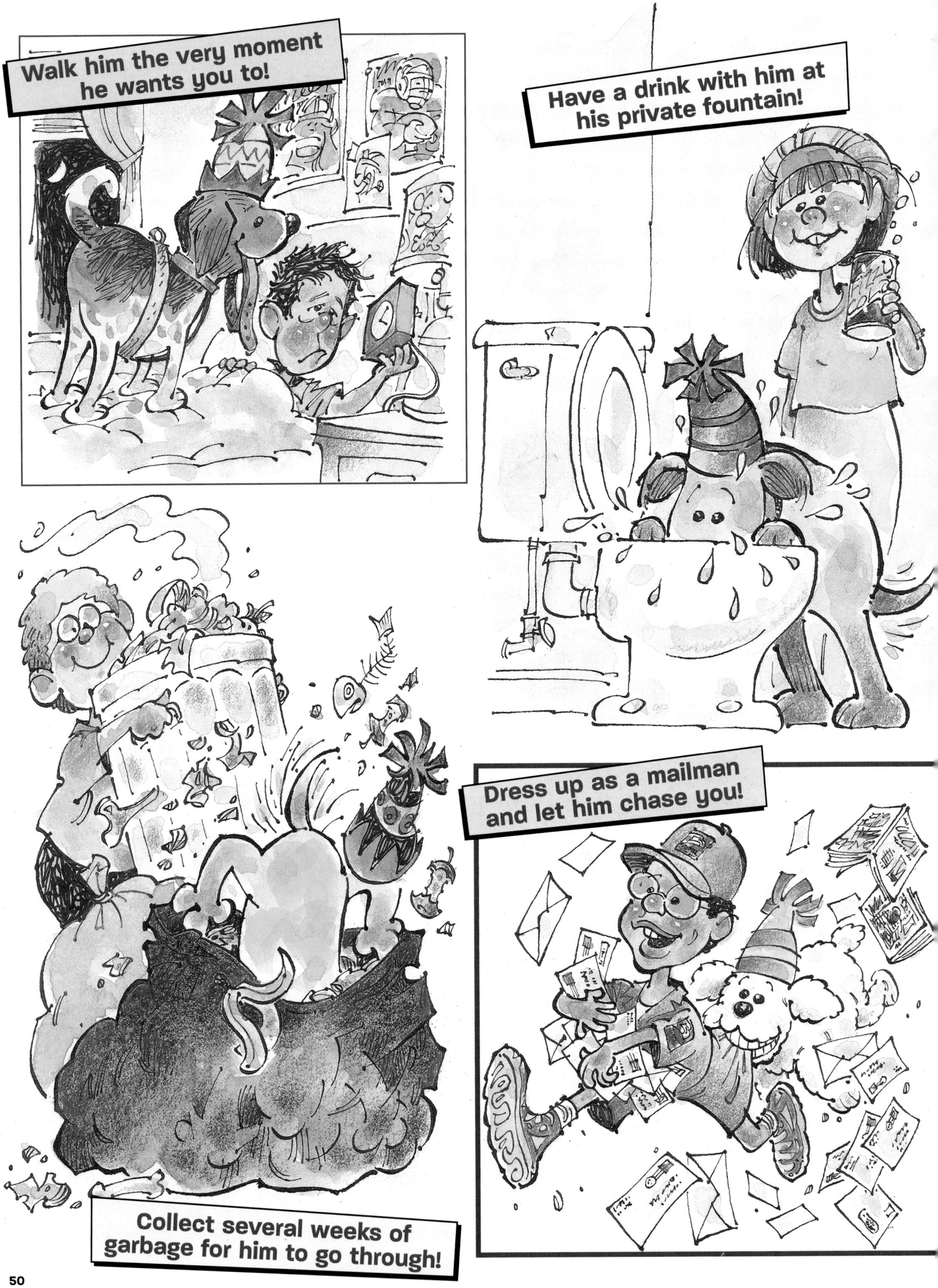

Walk him the very moment he wants you to!

Have a drink with him at his private fountain!

Collect several weeks of garbage for him to go through!

THE CONTINUING ADVENTURES OF WILLY NILLY

WRITER: MO WILLEMS ARTIST: JACOB CHABOT

JACOB CHABOT

Just pick a different item from each row as you read your way down the page and you'll have a ridiculous new SpongeBob episode every time!

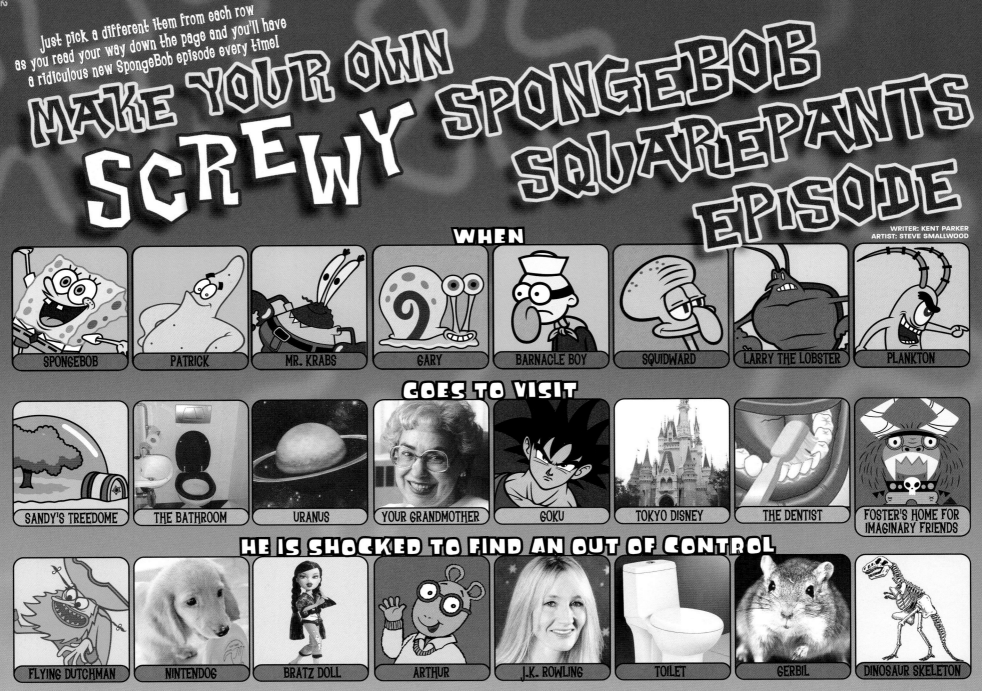

MAKE YOUR OWN SCREWY SPONGEBOB SQUAREPANTS EPISODE

WRITER: KENT PARKER
ARTIST: STEVE SMALLWOOD

WHEN

SPONGEBOB | PATRICK | MR. KRABS | GARY | BARNACLE BOY | SQUIDWARD | LARRY THE LOBSTER | PLANKTON

GOES TO VISIT

SANDY'S TREEDOME | THE BATHROOM | URANUS | YOUR GRANDMOTHER | GOKU | TOKYO DISNEY | THE DENTIST | FOSTER'S HOME FOR IMAGINARY FRIENDS

HE IS SHOCKED TO FIND AN OUT OF CONTROL

FLYING DUTCHMAN | NINTENDOG | BRATZ DOLL | ARTHUR | J.K. ROWLING | TOILET | GERBIL | DINOSAUR SKELETON

MERMAIDMAN
LONG DIVISION
THE OLSEN TWINS
A PICKLE JAR
ELMO
A RUNNY NOSE
THE CHICKENPOX
AN ITCHY SWEATER
AND THREATENING THE WORLD WITH
POISONOUS SEA URCHINS
TARTAR SAUCE
DIARRHEA
SUMMER SCHOOL
TOENAIL FUNGUS
A SPANKING
"CAN YOU HEAR ME NOW?" COMMERCIALS
CLONE TROOPERS
BUT WITH THE HELP OF
PAINTY THE PIRATE
ADAM SANDLER
KIM POSSIBLE
KING KONG
MARIO
DRAKE AND JOSH
THE GHOST OF ELVIS
THE FORCE
EVERYONE GOES ON A SCAVENGER HUNT WHERE THE PRIZE IS
THE SECRET KRABBY PATTY RECIPE
LUNCH WITH QUEEN LATIFAH
CLEAN UNDERWEAR
PEACE ON EARTH
HARRY POTTER'S WAND
ACCORDION LESSONS
AN XBOX 360
A METALLIC OUTER SHELL
AND THEY ALL END UP LIVING
IN A PINEAPPLE UNDER THE SEA
IN MINNESOTA
IN OUTER SPACE
AT TITANS TOWER
NEXT DOOR TO YOU
TO REGRET IT
IN AN IGLOO
IN THE WHITE HOUSE

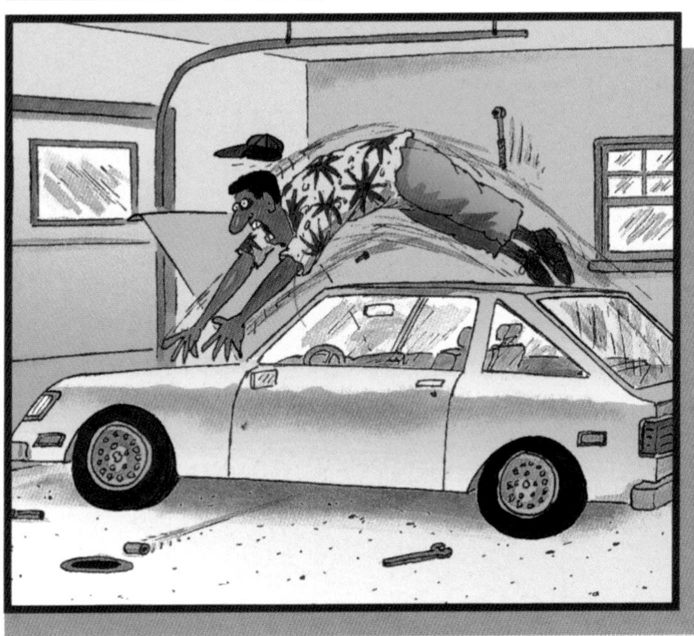

The **more** you paid for a socket wrench, the **faster** it will roll towards the garage floor drain when dropped.

A tire that goes flat on a high-speed expressway will **always** be located on the driver's side of the car.

AS A PUBLIC SERVICE, MAD IS OFFERING SOME TIPS FOR ALL YOU AUTO ENTHUSIASTS WHO LIKE TO PUT ON YOUR COVERALLS, GET UNDER THE HOOD

THE CAST IRON LA

WRITER AND ARTIST: TOM CHENEY

Virtually **any** part you remove from a car parked on a sloped driveway will be directly connected to the emergency brake system.

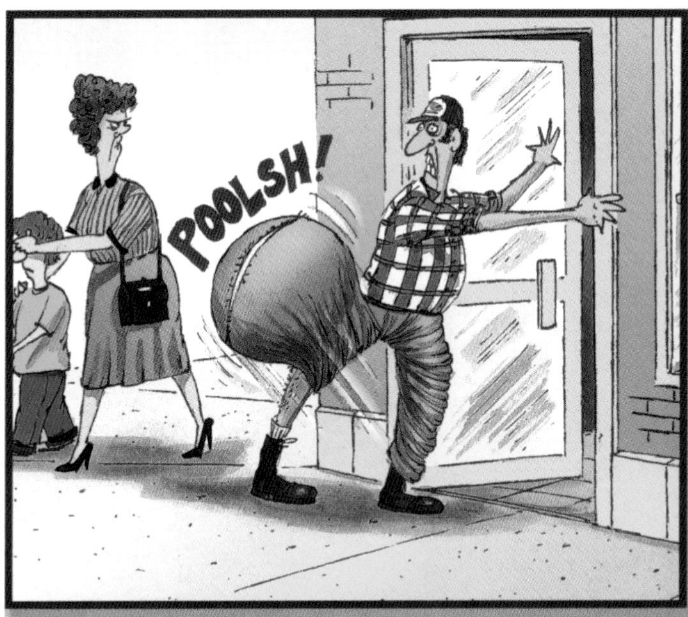

An airbag that fails to inflate during a collision will **always** inflate when you attempt to carry it back to the auto parts store in your pocke

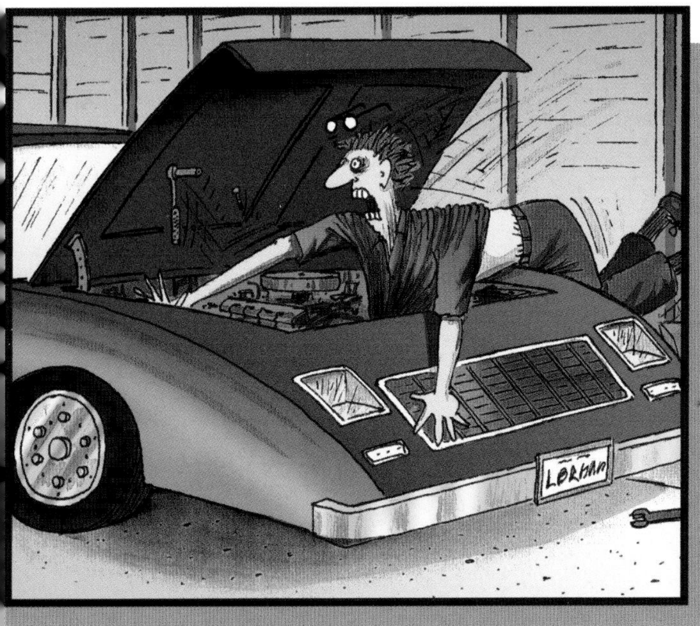

A part that can only be adjusted while the engine is running will **always** be located one inch or less from a spinning fan belt.

A horn that never works will **refuse** to shut itself off if you attempt to repair it after 2:00 a.m.

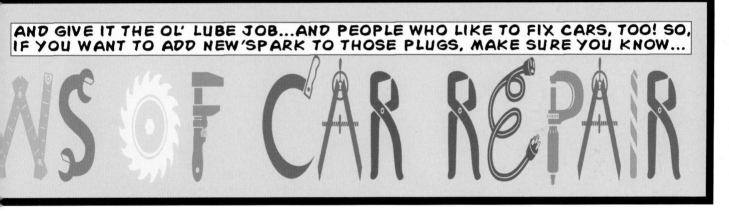

AND GIVE IT THE OL' LUBE JOB...AND PEOPLE WHO LIKE TO FIX CARS, TOO! SO, IF YOU WANT TO ADD NEW SPARK TO THOSE PLUGS, MAKE SURE YOU KNOW...

...WS OF CAR REPAIR

When you traveled to England last month you decided to pull out all the stops and go first class — so you had beef for dinner every night...Aren't *you* the genius!

The least expensive and most frequently replaced part on your car can **never** be reached without first removing the entire engine.

A grease gun will never accidentally discharge, **unless** it's pointed at an open car window.

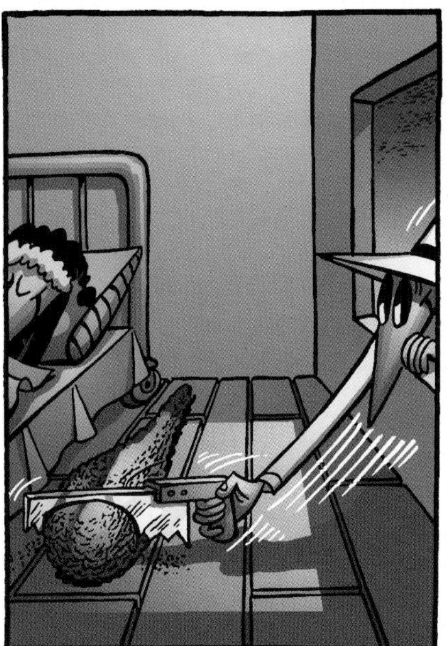

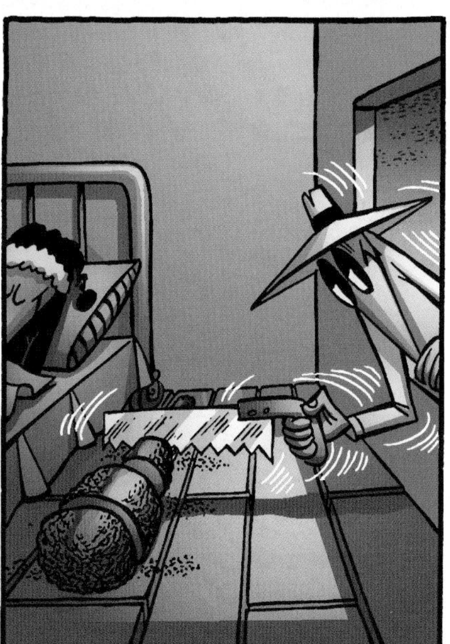

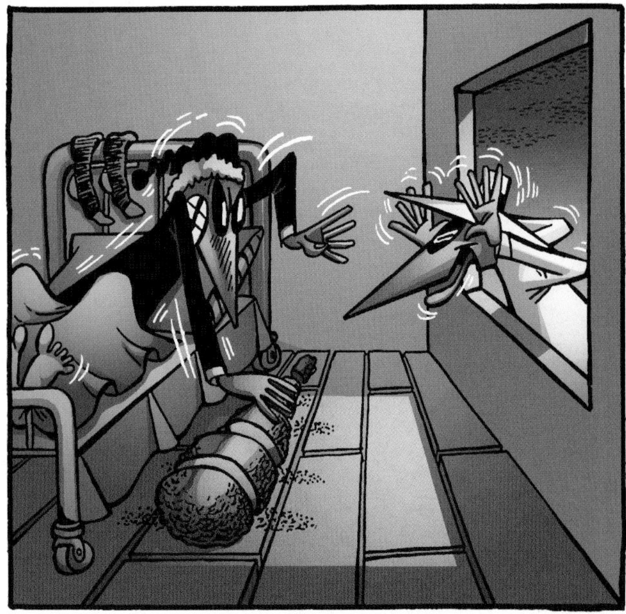

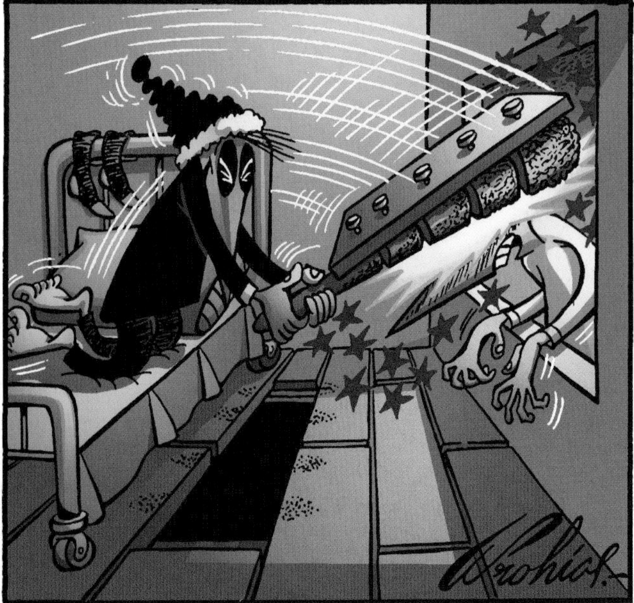

WRITER AND ARTIST: ANTONIO PROHIAS COLORIST: CARRIE STRACHAN

There are some wonderful books that have been around for 40 years and are loved by all. The following isn't one of them! Hold your nose, it's...

THE BIG POT OF BEANS

Mr. And Mrs. Rumproast were just getting home from their jobs when their younger son, Arthur, called from the bedroom he shared with his brother, Stanley.

"Hey! Come and look! Hey!"

Mr. And Mrs. Rumproast rushed to the bedroom and saw Stanley lying on his bed.

"Is he sick?" asked Mrs. Rumproast.

"Give it a few seconds," answered Arthur.

And indeed, in just five seconds, the room was filled with a loud "Poooot!" sound and Stanley raised four feet above his bed. Then, Mr. and Mrs. Rumproast realized that the room was also filled with a nasty, nasty smell.

"Ewww!" yelled Mr. Rumproast. "What crawled up inside of you and died?"

"Today at school they served beans for lunch. None of the other students wanted any, so I ate the entire pot," answered Stanley.

"It was a 10-gallon pot," added Arthur.

"He's flatulent!" said Mrs. Rumproast, having just opened the bedroom window as much as it would open.

"Flat-you-what?" asked Arthur.

Mrs. Rumproast tried to explain. "He's gassy, uh, colicky…"

"She means I can't stop farting," said Stanley as he again broke wind and with a long "Frrpppt!" rose three feet off the bed.

"What can we do?" Said Mr. Rumproast.

"I know what I'm going to do," said Arthur. "As long as Stanley keeps cutting the cheese, I'm going to sleep in the living room! Pew!"

And for once, Arthur's parents agreed with him.

THE STUDENTS GET WIND OF STANLEY

On the first day back at school after Stanley ate the big pot of beans, the other students could sense there was something different in the air, even before Stanley arrived.

"Do you smell something funny?" asked Trevor. "Yes, it smells like a big clog at the sewage plant," said Jasmine.

"Look!" shouted Benjamin, as he pointed down the street. All the students saw what he was pointing at: Stanley could be seen rising up above the trees, lifted by what looked like a greenish-brown cloud. When Stanley and Arthur arrived in the school yard, all the students surrounded him — at first.

"Stanley, why were you floating in the air?" asked Stephan. "I'm flatulent," answered Stanley, as his parents had instructed him to do.

"Flat WHAT?" said Tom. "I think that means he makes smelly blurps" said Emily. "No," interrupted Trevor, "it means he fires off air biscuits." Benjamin said, "Stanley means he has belly bombs." "You know what Stanley has now?" riddled Jasmine. "A butt bugle!"

"What he means," said Arthur, "is that he farts. Big."

Just then, Stanley went "Fraffffft!" and raised several feet above the schoolyard. All the students ran away screaming, choking and holding their noses. Stanley had just learned another new word: unpopular.

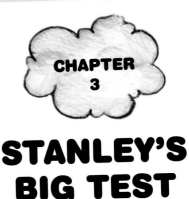

STANLEY'S BIG TEST

When class started, Stanley sat on one side of the room and all the other students sat on the other side of the room, in case Stanley cut a big ripper.

Just then, the teacher, Mrs. Toomey, entered the room. "Class, today I'm giving you a surprise 100-question quiz." The students moaned as Mrs. Toomey began handing out the test papers.

Suddenly, Stanley had an idea. None of the

9

teachers knew yet that he was now Flatulent Stanley.

After putting his finger to his mouth to warn the other students to be quiet, he pushed against the back of his seat and released a huge silent-but-deadly cloud.

"What's that foul smell?" asked Mrs. Toomey. "It smells like the gas pipes might be leaking," said Benjamin, playing along with Stanley.

"Eww! It smells like an explosion at the sauerkraut factory!" said Mrs. Toomey. "Class, line up and leave the school, I'm reporting this to the Principal!"

Mrs. Toomey told the Principal, who also smelled the foul, gassy cloud. Together they spoke to all the students, now lined up outside the school. "I'm sorry, but until we find out what the

10

smell is, I won't be able to give the quiz," said Mrs. Toomey. "In fact, it smells so bad in there I'm calling off school for the rest of the day," added the Principal. As the students ran home, a cheer went up. Stanley, you're the hero of the whole school," said Emily. With another cheer, the students raised Stanley and began carrying him on their shoulders. That ended one loud "Fuurrrt!" later.

THE ROTTEN ROYAL RUSE

Your Majesty! You can't RAISE the TAXES again! Your subjects are so poor that many have taken to the streets to beg!
NONSENSE! You make it out to be WORSE than it is! I will GO OUT and see for MYSELF what they think of their KING!

But, Sire! THINK of the DANGER!
Don't be a FOOL! I will be DISGUISED as one of their own! They will NEVER KNOW their KING walks AMONG THEM!

YOUR HIGHNESS! Your DISGUISE is AMAZING! If I didn't know you to be the KING, I'd believe you to be a BEGGAR in the STREETS!
HAH! If YOU can be CONVINCED Gunther, then surely no lowly BEGGAR will SUSPECT my TRUE IDENTITY! Please get my HAT!

WRITER AND ARTIST: DUCK EDWING

HEY, guys! I really do LOVE our KING! WHAT do YOU THINK about HIM?
PLEASE

ARE
A S

Are you lacking a little in the personal hygiene department? Do you take a bath once a month, whether you think you need it or not? Has a government agency ever ordered the evacuation of your room fearing a massive "junk avalanche?" Then perhaps you should spend the next few minutes taking the following MAD quiz...

You start with 100 points. Add additional points after each question.

1) For every slice of pizza your mother finds when she makes your bed ....**ADD 3**

2) If your mother has to use an ice scraper o
your clothes before washing them....**ADD 5**
A jackhammer.............................**ADD 15**

3) For every pet who has ever "gone missing" in your room
ADD 20

4) If the pile of dirty laundry in your room joined the Great Wall of China and the Pyramids as the only man-made objects visible from space
ADD 10

5) If, when having a sleepover, your friend's parents insist on them wearing bio-hazard suit
before entering your room................**ADD 10**

YOU
LOB?

WRITER: J. PRETE
ARTIST: JOHNNY RYAN

6) If your room was near the center of a massive earthquake and mudslide, and it looked the same after the quake was over..........**ADD 10**

7) If you can write your name in the dust on your furniture........**ADD 5**

If you can write the name of every kid in your class..........**ADD 10**

Every kid in your school...........**ADD 20**

8) If there is enough dirt under your fingernails to grow a small tomato plant **ADD 5**

9) If you put on a clean shirt every morning..................**ADD 0**

If you put on the shirt that stinks the least..............**ADD 5**

If the question doesn't apply to you because you usually wear the same clothes you slept in......**ADD 10**

10) If you spent an hour rooting through all your junk trying to find a pencil to take this test **ADD 10**

If you scored more than 115, you're a real super slob!
If you scored less than 115, you're a regular slob!
Either way, you're a slob!

JUST A PHRASE WE'RE GOING THROUGH DEPT.

Several issues back, we astutely pointed out to you the true UNimportance of words in every-day life. It is not the words that are significant, we explained, so much as the particular context in which the words are used. Judging by the letters we received after publishing this

MORE SAME WORDS... *DIFFE*

I PICKED IT THIS MORNING!

...is okay when discussing fruits and vegetables.

...not okay for just about anything else!

HE'S GOT H

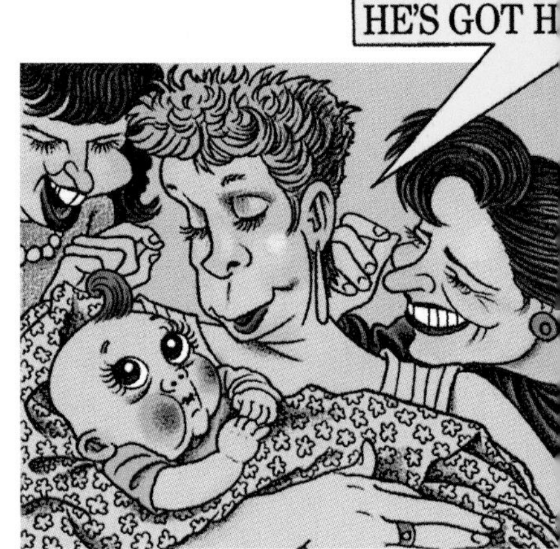

...is cute when cuddling a newborn.

COLD AND CLOUDY!

...is fine when describing today's weather.

...revolting when describing your school cafeteria's soup du jour!

FI

...is expected when pumping gas is your job.

SNAP, CRACKLE, POP!

...is pleasant when it's the sound made by your cereal every morning.

...unpleasant when it's the sound made by your body every morning!

I'M OU

...is bad news when it's your father or mother.

article, we came to the conclusion that you applauded this amazingly clever and bold observa-
ion (although our conclusion could change once we actually get around to reading those three
etters)! In any event, using *different* words and *different* circumstances, we now present...

RENT CIRCUMSTANCES!

WRITER: J. PRETE ARTIST: RICK TULKA COLORIST: CARL PETERSON

...a tad disturbing when hiding from a psychotic homicidal maniac!

EAT MY SHORTS!

...is funny when Bart Simpson yells it at his Mom and Dad.

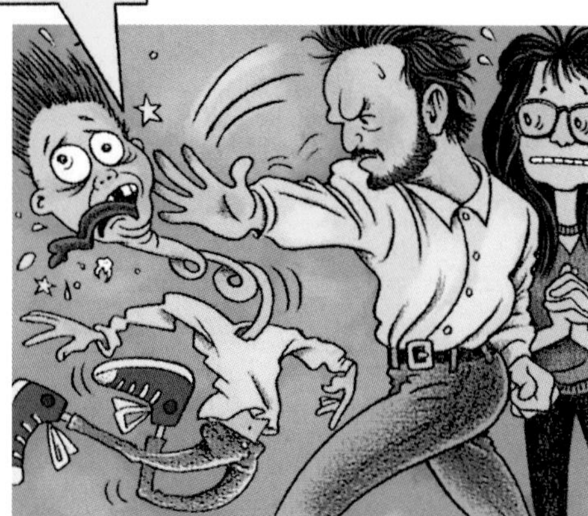

...not so funny when you yell it at yours!

R UP!

...insulting when you are applying for a job!

...is no problem when buying a soda.

...a big problem when buying a bra!

...great news when it's one of the Senators involved in the Savings and Loan Scandal!

TWO DOWN AND THREE ACROSS ARE ALL YOU HAVE LEFT!

...is fine when describing the last clues to a crossword puzzle.

...not so fine when a dentist is describing your last remaining teeth!

DON MARTIN DEPT.

DON MARTIN BEATS THE

HIGH COST OF GASOLINE

WRITER AND ARTIST: DON MARTIN

WATER
AIR COND.

WATER
KLIK
VROOM
SPOOSH

WATER

MARBLE SHOOTING CHAMPIONSHIP

SPRAY CANS MADE TO ORDER

PSSSH

BIRD VITAMINS

D. MARTIN..

THE DWAYNE CHRONICLES

WRITER AND ARTIST: ERIC SCOTT

WRITER AND ARTIST: PAUL PETER PORGE

LOOK AT TS' TALK

COLORIST: CARRIE STRACHAN

If you like THIS BOOK, be sure to check out our OTHER PUBLICATIONS shown here!

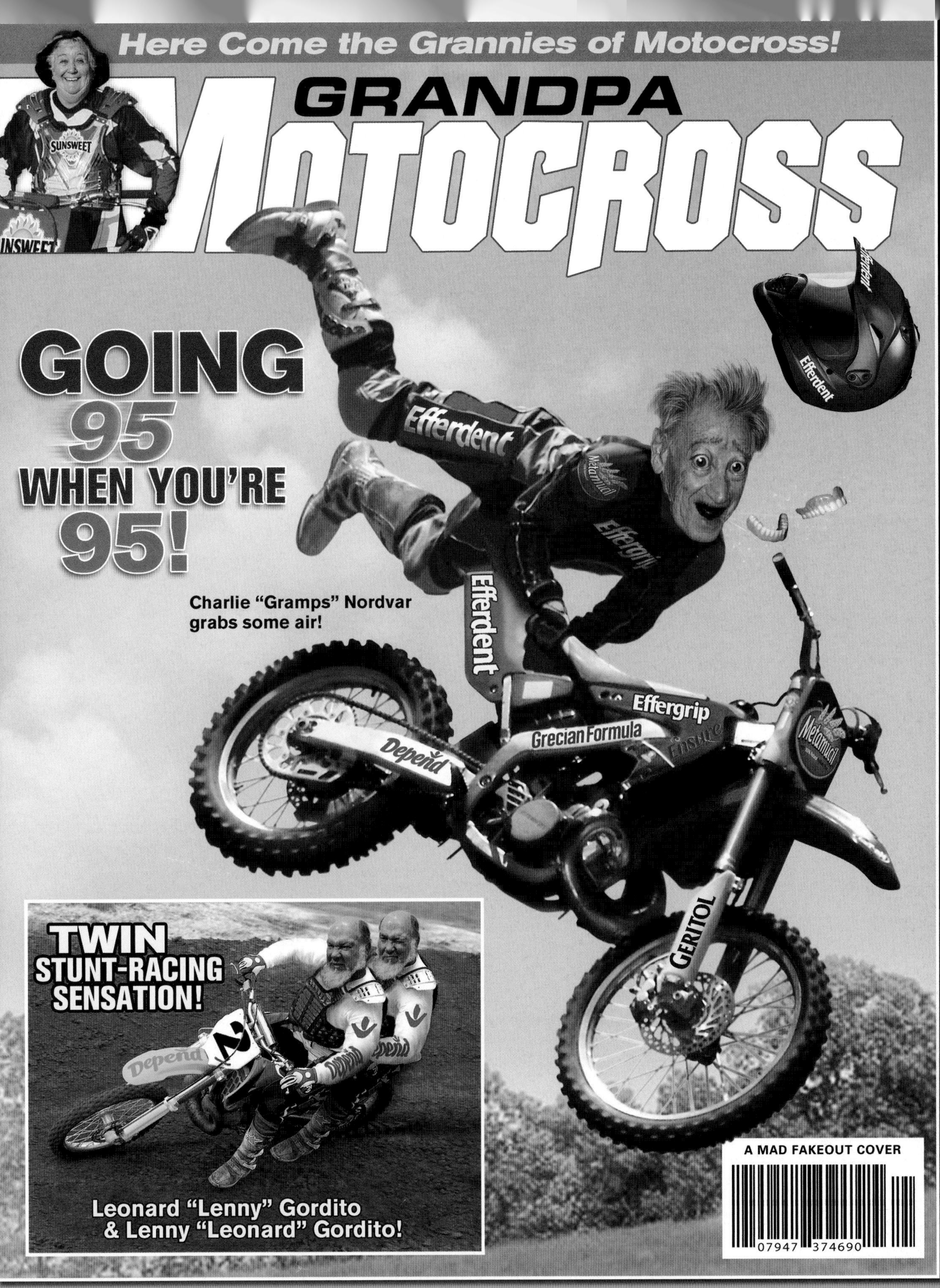
Here Come the Grannies of Motocross!
GRANDPA
MOTOCROSS
SUNSWEET
GOING
95
WHEN YOU'RE
95!
Charlie "Gramps" Nordvar
grabs some air!
Efferdent
Effergrip
Efferdent
Effergrip
Grecian Formula
Depend
Ensure
Metamucil
GERITOL
TWIN
STUNT-RACING
SENSATION!
Depend
Leonard "Lenny" Gordito
& Lenny "Leonard" Gordito!
A MAD FAKEOUT COVER
07947 374690

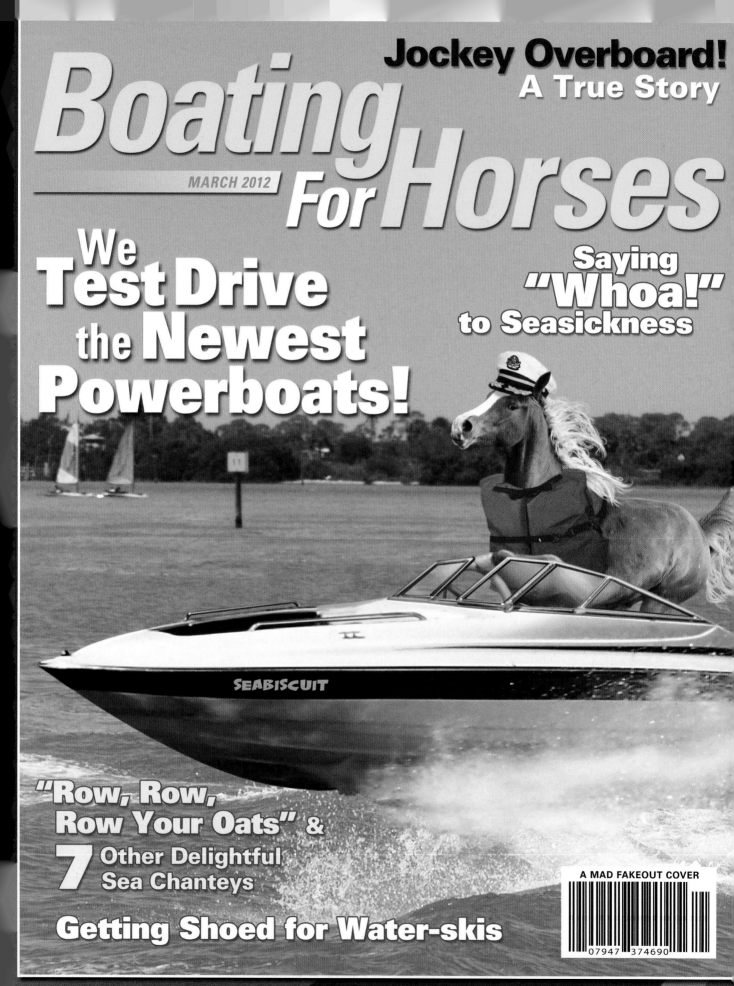

Jockey Overboard!
A True Story

Boating For Horses

MARCH 2012

We Test Drive the Newest Powerboats!

Saying "Whoa!" to Seasickness

"Row, Row, Row Your Oats" & 7 Other Delightful Sea Chanteys

Getting Shoed for Water-skis

>>> NEW HEAD LICE MERIT BADGE PLANNED SEE PAGE 9

Boys' Lice

WHERE SCOUTING AND INFESTATION MEET

TURN YOUR HEAD INTO A HATCHERY... ...IT'S EASY!

PAGE 22

Training your nits to do **TRICKS!**

Share hats with your friends and have a **LICE DAY!**

$3.60

A MAD FAKEOUT COVER

Fairy Tale
SCENES WE'D LIKE TO SEE
THE FROG PRINCE

WRITER AND ARTIST: DON MARTIN

SERGIO ARAGONÉS PRESENTS A MAD LOOK AT PRICE CLUBS

WRITER AND ARTIST: SERGIO ARAGONÉS COLORIST: TOM LUTH

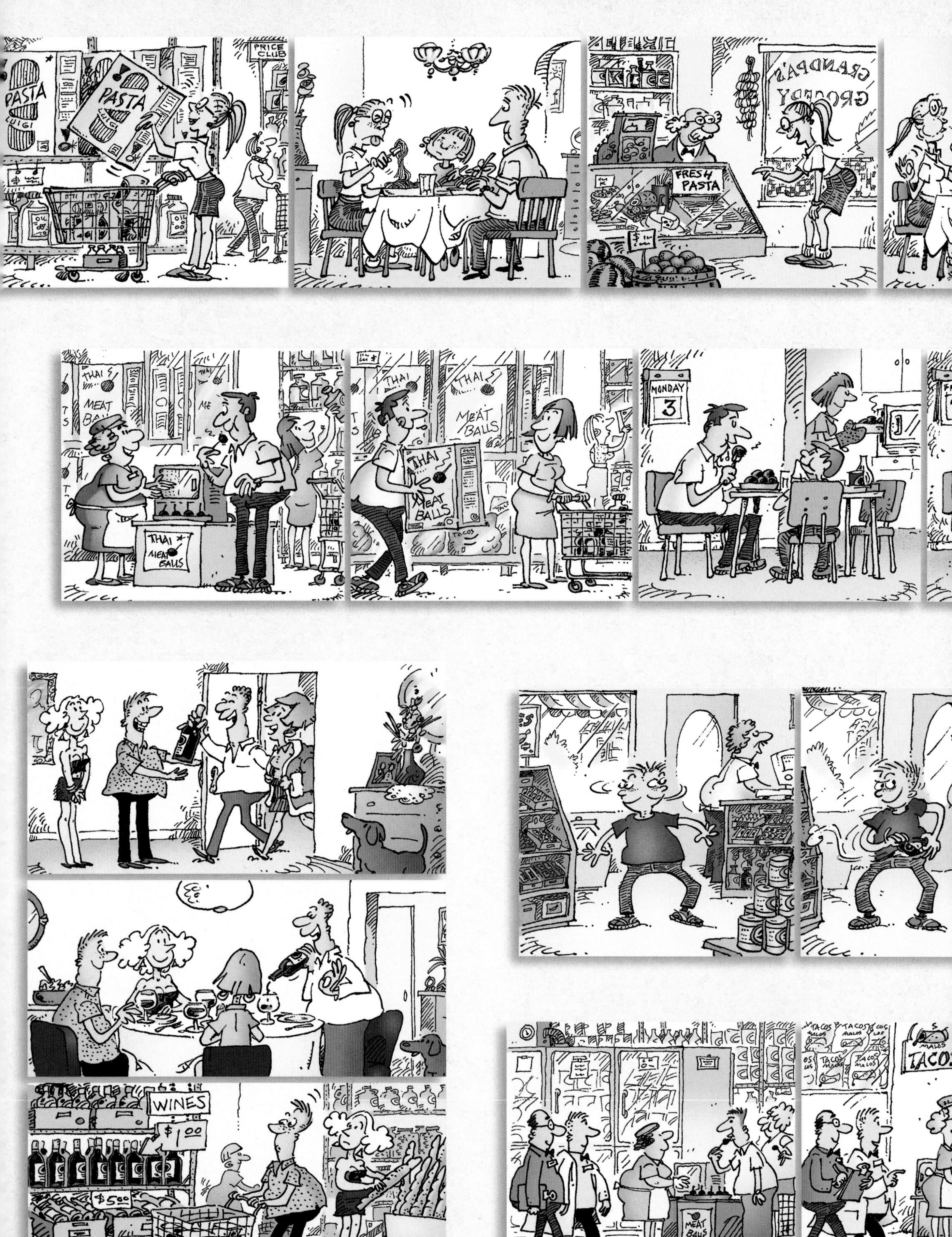
PASTA
LUIGI
PASTA
LUIGI
PRICE CLUB
OIL
GRANDPA'S GROCERY
FRESH PASTA
THAI
MEAT BALLS
THAI
MEAT BALLS
THAI
MEAT BALLS
THAI
MEAT BALLS
TACOS
MONDAY
3
WINES
$1.00
$5.00
TACOS MALOS
TACOS
MEAT BALLS

CHICKEN
CASSEROLE
CHICKEN
CASSEROLE
CHICKEN
CASSEROLE

BUTCHER
COMING SOON!
PRICE CLUB
MAYONNAIS 
CRACKERS
DETERGENT
FAB
NEW!
ARAGONÉS

SPY VS SPY

GLUE
BUS STOP

GLUE
BUS STOP
CLICK

GLUE
BUS STOP

GLUE
BUS STOP

GLUE
BUS STOP

Prohías

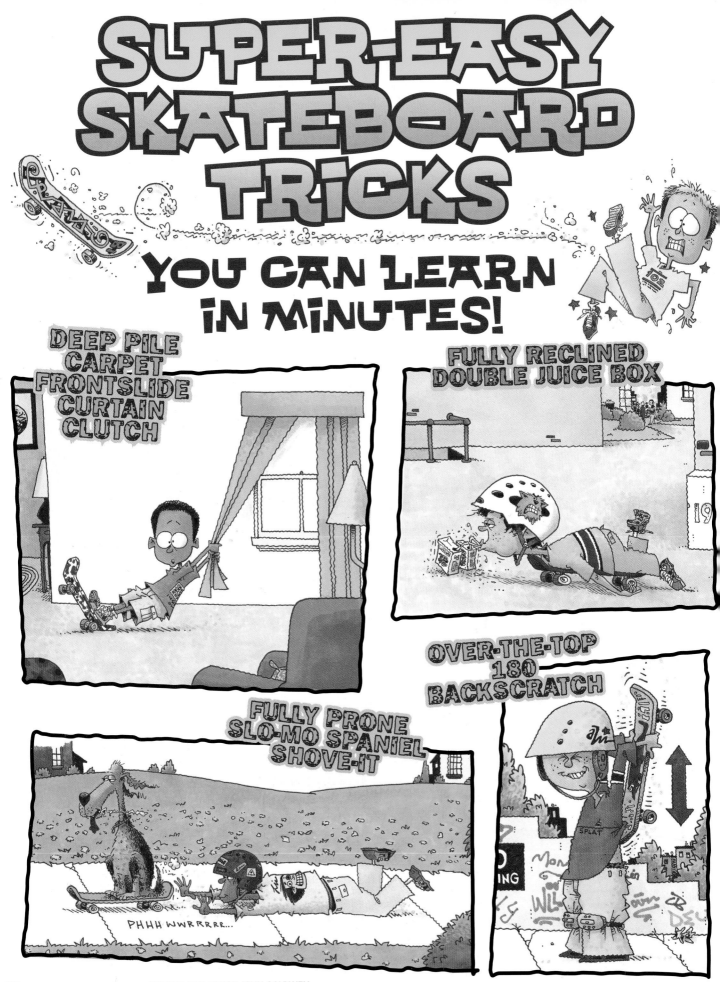

SUPER-EASY SKATEBOARD TRICKS

YOU CAN LEARN IN MINUTES!

DEEP PILE CARPET FRONTSLIDE CURTAIN CLUTCH

FULLY RECLINED DOUBLE JUICE BOX

OVER-THE-TOP 180 BACKSCRATCH

FULLY PRONE SLO-MO SPANIEL SHOVE-IT

WRITER AND ARTIST: JOHN CALDWELL

BANNISTER BALANCE BREAK, PIVOT AND CRINGE
ZZZWIZZZZZZZZZZZZ
PA PWAK!
PATWISSHHH
BWUF
TINKLE
TINK

FRONTSIDE DOUBLE KNEE STATIONARY CALCULATOR TAP
TAP
TAP
TAPPA
TAP
TAP...

FULL VERTICAL MARVIN
KRIK.
KRIK
KRIK...

MODIFIED DRIVEWAY BACKSIDE BUTT BUSTER AND SIDE WINDOW SMASH COMBO
TWAAAAAAAAASSH!!!
102-T

FRESHLY POLISHED COFFEE TABLE POWERSLIDE AND NOSEGRIND

MAIM THAT TUNE DEPT.

Each year, millions of tiny kids are herded into day care centers and Sunday schools where they are commanded to join in the singing of traditional songs and carols before they are old enough to read and understand the lyrics. The result is tragically predictable. They sing the words they think they hear, and form a pattern that often lasts a lifetime. Many preoccupied grownups keep right on singing the same muddled words to the same songs in the same way. This, of course, makes us sound like a nation of idiots as we stand reverently at such somber events as patriotic rallies, church services and even baseball games to fill the air with …

AMERICA'S T

AS THEY SOUND

My Uncle, Liz And Me

My uncle, Liz and me

Eat ham with liberty.
Of tea, we sing.

Ham that my father fried;
Ham when the children cried.

On every mountainside,
Let's clean 'til Spring.

The Star Strangled Grandma

No way can you see through this song's early light
What had sounded like hail at the night light's loud screamin

Who brought tripe and Mars bars to the last Eastern flight
On the rampage with scotch while the gals were all steaming

And our pockets were bare
When they first hit the air
As they proved we were right and our bags were still there.

No way does that star strangled Grandma smell Dave,
For the mandolin is free,
And our home is a cave.

RADITIONAL SONGS TO FIVE-YEAR-OLDS

WRITER: TOM KOCH ARTIST: PAUL COKER COLORIST: CARRIE STRACHAN

That Marine! Him!

From the Halls of Minneso-ota
To the doors of misery,

We will ride on grumpy ca-attle
In Iran and Italy.

If the Army or the Navy
Ever look at magazines,

They will find the creeps with garden tools
Have been smashed to smithereens.

America, The Boot Is Full

Your boot is full of spacey guys,
And candles made by Jane,

From curdled mounds of macramé
Above the flutes in Spain.

America! America! Go shed your grapes on me.

Your clown's no good at motherhood.
We'll see what we shall see.

IN A FANCY RESTAURANT

WRITER AND ARTIST: DON MARTIN COLORIST: CARL PETERSON

SCOTT NICKEL

THE COMIC WITH NO NAME

MO WILLEMS

DUSTIN GLICK

JOEY ALISON SAYERS

PONDERING THE REALLY MEANINGFUL STUFF

IT IS A QUESTION THAT HAS TROUBLED THE GREATEST MINDS OF OUR TIME...

HOW DOES ONE **SPELL** THE SOUND OF A FART?

GOD IN HEAVEN, THERE **MUST** BE A WAY!

MANY HAVE TRIED... ALL HAVE FAILED.

SOUNDED LIKE "POOT."

I HEARD "FERNT."

GIVE US ANOTHER, PAUL.

IN THE LATE FIFTIES, A CARTOONIST NAMED ALVIN JOHNSON CAME CLOSE...

FPLBLXPZ.

EUREKA!

...BUT HIS "FPLBLXPZ THEOREM" WAS ULTIMATELY PROVEN FALSE BY A STANFORD AUDIO TECH IN LATE 1969.

MY TAPES HAVE REVEALED A DISTINCTLY UN-FPLBLXPZ-ISH SOUND!

WHATEVER, DUDE. THAT MICROPHONE **REEKS**!

ONOMATOPOEIA EXPERT PIP BINGBONG EXPLAINS THE DILEMMA.

THE PROBLEM IS OUR LIMITED ALPHABET. WE NEED A NEW LETTER. SOMETHING LIKE "∝."

HARRELL

WHAT WILL IT TAKE? A NEW ALPHABET? SOME SORT OF SUPER COMPUTER? SMARTER HUMANS?

COULD THE GREAT THINKER THAT WILL CRACK THIS SPHINXIAN RIDDLE BE... **YOU?**

ROB HARRELL

ME, MYSELF AND MY PUPPET

AT THE STORE

JOHN KOVALESKI

AFTER DECADES OF PREPARATION, THE FIENDISH **DOCTOR DISASTER** UNLEASHES HIS 30-STORY-HIGH SOLID STEEL MONSTER!

TED RALL

TALES FROM THE DUCK SIDE DEPT.

The Outrageous Orchestral Offense

ARTIST AND WRITER: DUCK EDWING

ARTIST: SCOTT BRICHER

GAMEPRO
CHEAT CODES
VIDEO GAME
A MAD POSTER

Planet TAD!!!!!

http://www.galaxyo'blogs.com/planettad

Search

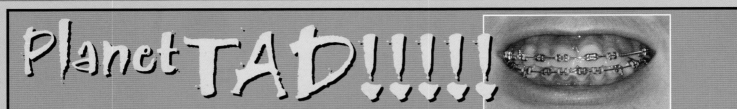

Planet TAD!!!!!

[16 October|**11:33am**]

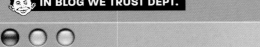

[**mood**| whatever]

Chet and I went to the movies last night and saw Flightplan, that new movie about how Jodie Foster loses her daughter on an airplane.

* * * * Spoiler Alert!!!!!! * * * * *

It stinks.

[17 October|**03:14pm**]

D.J., the driver of my school bus, is a big fan of the Tasmanian Devil. He's got Tasmanian Devil shirts, and hats, and has a Tasmanian Devil tattooed on his arm. He acts like it makes him cool, but who really cares about the Tasmanian Devil once they're older than like eight years old? If I got a tattoo, it would have to be something I really knew I was going to care about forever, like Natalie Portman.

[19 October|**07:54pm**]

I've got a social studies test tomorrow that I have to study for. My social studies textbook is hard to read because it's all about how important it is to participate in democracy and be proud of your country, but it's really old — like, from the '70s — and it's been illustrated with photos like this one:

November 2, 1976. Jimmy Carter's supporters

These are the worst spokespeople for voting ever. As my friend Darren put it, "It looks like the people of Lameville are getting a new mayor."

[20 October|**04:03pm**]

[**mood**| psyched]

A while ago, Chet and Darren and I started playing poker at lunch, using all the tricks we've learned from watching Celebrity Poker Showdown. (I'm kind of a Brad Garrett-type player. Chet's more of a Jason Alexander. Darren said he was a Bonnie Hunt-type player, but then we started calling him "Bonnie" and he denied he'd ever said it.) We don't play for money or anything — just for packets of ketchup and mustard. We used to just play for ketchup, but then we started playing "no-limits", and so we decided that mustard packets are worth five ketchup packets. But lately Chet's been betting big, and we're thinking of making relish worth five mustards.

Anyway, Billy Otis, who's a senior, came over and watched for a few minutes. He said that we're all really good players, and that we should come to the game he hosts with his friends every Friday night in his basement. So we're going to get a chance to play for real. I'm pretty psyched, because I generally tend to clean up with the ketchup packets, and I figure if I do well tomorrow, I can take the $50 I've been saving for the new Madden game for my PS2 and turn it into enough to buy an Xbox 360, Game Boy Micro AND the new Madden game.

[22 October|**10:26am**]

[**mood**|  bummed]

Too depressed to blog.

[22 October|**02:17pm**]

[**mood**|  totally bummed]

Still too depressed to blog. But if you want to buy a PlayStation 2 on eBay, there's one for sale here.

Also, there's a bunch of PlayStation games for sale here.

Also, a whole lot of near-mint-condition comic books for sale here.

And a bike here.

Please bid high. I need to make $300 by Friday.

[25 October|**03:49pm**]

Does anyone know how to mail a bike?

ARTIST: BRIAN DURNIAK PHOTO: AP/WIDEWORLD PHOTOS WRITER: TIM CARVELL

THE CONTINUING ADVENTURES OF WILLY NILLY

WRITER: JOHN CALDWELL ARTIST: JACOB CHABOT

STANKEE CANDLE

Spring Catalog

Over 50
Unmistakable Odors!

Our Newest Aroma,
Flatulent Pony —
It's Like Taking an
Ankle-Deep Stroll Through
a Kentucky Meadow!

STANKEE CANDLE
FLATULENT PONY

New Scents
That Will
Take Your
Breath Away...

...Perhaps
Forever!

Haunting Newcomers

Morning's Breath

You'll swear your face is still drool-glued to the pillow when this rich, breathy bouquet fills the room. This evocative product instantly conjures the pasty, mucousy mysteries of sleep…any time of the day!

Chain Smoker's Cottage

Enjoy all the pleasures of nicotine addiction without the expense, as our slow-burning, tar-based candle brings back those halcyon days when the whole world was one big, happy smoking section! Alive with carcinogens!

Hospital Corridors

Recapture the peace and quiet you can only achieve while walking the hallways of your favorite ICU unit! This memorable scent features the hints of ammonia, processed meals and the musty breeze that dances through the opening at the back of your gown.

Home Swee Homeless Man

Now you can instantly enjoy the soul-warming feeling of dropping a dime in an indigent's cu The scents of blundere humanity and old-time piddle intermingle to form a vibrant medley guaranteed to awaken the senses.

Whispers of Haddock

What could be more relaxing than a day on the high seas? Close your eyes and enjoy the scents of the catch of the day, freshly trawled from the murky waters below. The refreshing aroma of hot sea air blowing over a net full of flailing haddock can rejuvenate the soul!

Unforgettable Aromas

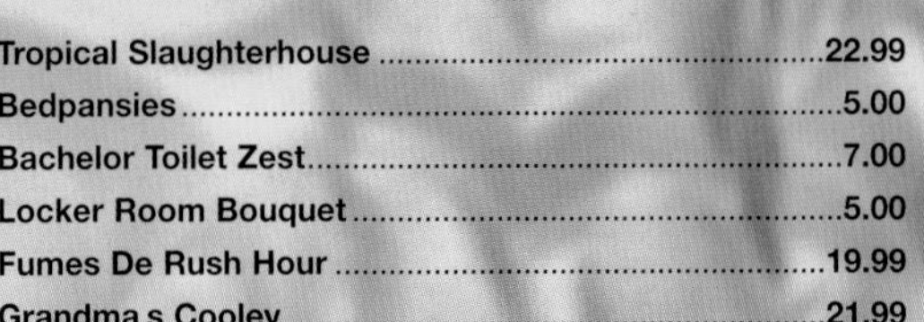

Tropical Slaughterhouse	22.99
Bedpansies	5.00
Bachelor Toilet Zest	7.00
Locker Room Bouquet	5.00
Fumes De Rush Hour	19.99
Grandma s Cooley	21.99

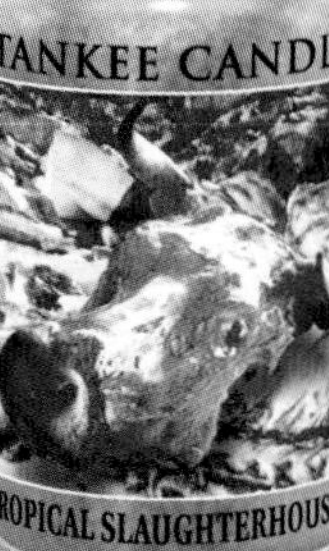

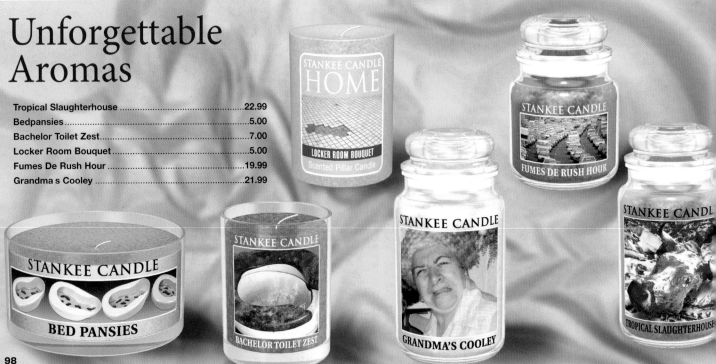

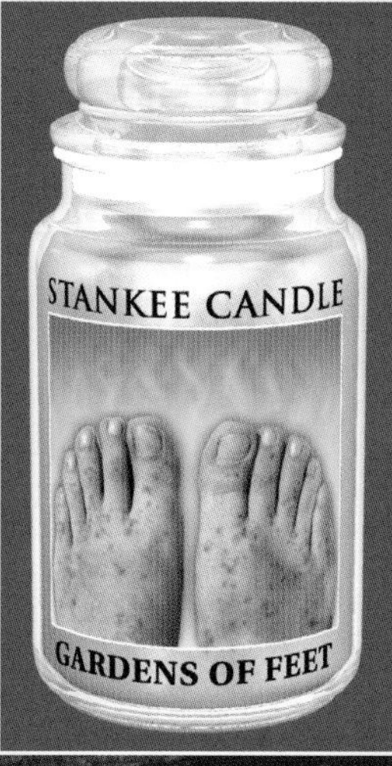

Our Body Part Collection

NEW! Autumn Leaves

Adult Diaper Medley	22.99
Gardens of Feet	22.99
Hot Stomach Rising	19.99
A Touch of Butt	22.99
Children s Fingers	22.99
Bloated Corpse Breeze	19.99

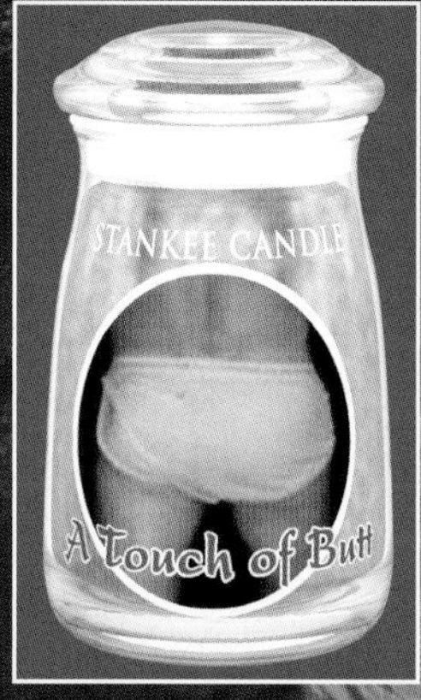

Children's Fingers

Recapture the sticky-skinned innocence of childhood with this pungently nostalgic aroma. Its strong, exceptionally true fragrance will instantly remind you of toddlers' stubby digits — still tacky from a day spent exploring the darkest corners of nature…and their own bodies.

Arresting Scents

Visit one of our many locations!

Or shop online at www.stankeecandle.con! (Because when you're spending $15 on a scented candle, who wants to actually smell it first?)But, whatever you do, keep buying candles instead of, you know, turning on a light or something!

WRITER: TERESA BURNS PARKHURST **ARTIST: SCOTT BRICHER** **PHOTOGRAPHER: IRVING SCHILD**

THE FANTASTIC

HAS A REALLY BAD WE

MONDAY

Always the practical joker, *MR. FANTASTIC* tells his nephew to pull his *FINGER*. Sadly, the kid is gone for days.

TUESDAY

The *FANTASTIC FOUR* spend *MILLIONS* to change their logo after *THE THING* quits. (A week later, he rejoins the group.)

THURSDAY

A delightful *PICNIC LUNCH* in the park is ruined for *THE THING* when a bunch of kids start up a game of *HANDBALL* on his back.

WRITERS: JOHNNY RYAN AND GREG LEITMAN ARTIST: JOHNNY RYAN

Once again, a visit to Baskin-Robbins ends in *HEARTACHE* for the *HUMAN TORCH*.

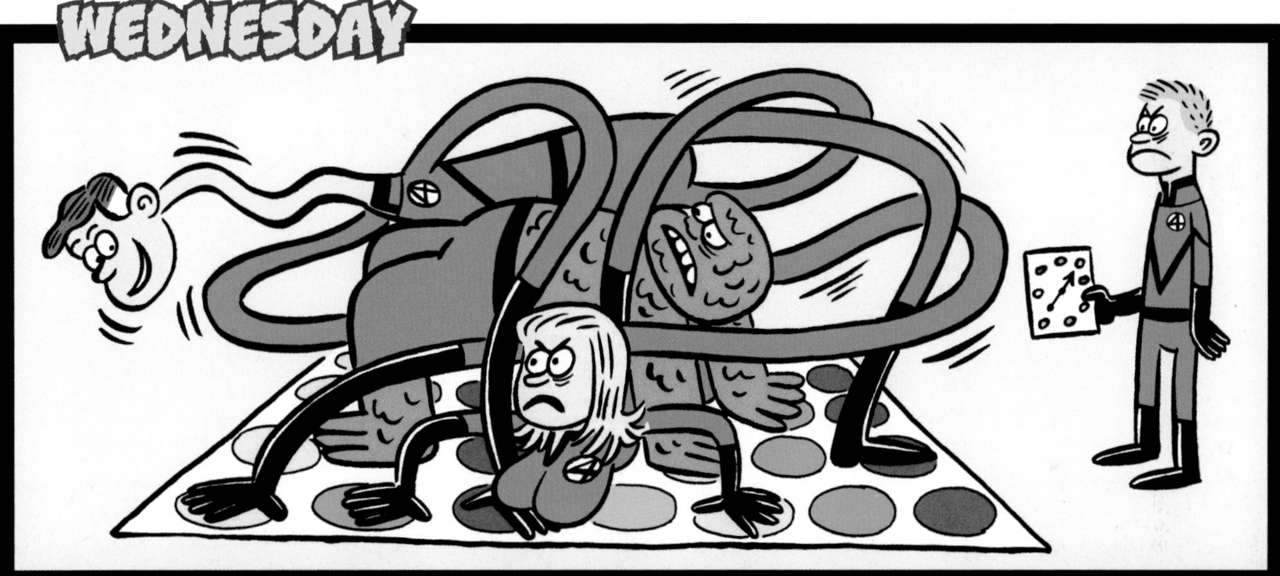

Tensions among the four rise when *MR. FANTASTIC* uses his *SPECIAL POWER* to win the weekly game of *TWISTER*.

MR. FANTASTIC is swiftly ejected from Yankee Stadium for *INTERFERING* with the game.

A group hug goes *HORRIBLY* wrong.

ONE THURSDAY AFTERNOON AT THE EDGE OF A MEADOW

WRITER: SERGIO ARAGONÉS ARTIST: DON MARTIN

HOCK AROUND THE CLOCK DEPT.
Have a piece of crap in the attic you think might be worth a fortune? You don't have to wait until Antiques Roadshow comes to your town. Just schlep it out to Vegas where four very laid-back people will check it out when, and if, they feel like it. We're talking about the...
YAWN Stars
I'm Slick Hair-is-Gone and this is my pawn shop! I work here with my old man and my son, Big Loss. There are three things I learned after 21 years in the pawn shop business. One, you never know what weird crap people are gonna drag in to try and sell. Well, actually we always know because the producers have pre-screened it to make sure it makes for a good episode! But play along for the sake of the show. Two, you never get over how easy it is to buy that crap and unload it on some sucker who thinks he's getting a bargain! And three, you never know how low The History Channel will sink to fill their schedule with ridiculous shows!
My son Slick owns the shop because I left it to him in my will! Technically I'm not dead, but I do so little around here that Slick just assumed I was and took over the shop! My main responsibilities are to annoy my son and my two-ton grandson and to take naps. I excel at my job!
EINSTEIN
SALE
WORLD FAMOUS JUNK YARD
TOM SHRUNK
I'm Big Loss! You're probably wondering why anyone in their right mind would visit a pawn shop in Las Vegas — the gambling capital of the world. Actually, that's why they visit us! These people are desperate! They've gambled away every buck so they have to sell their most treasured possessions to raise enough money to get home to their loved ones. Once you realize that, you'll agree that my father, grandfather and I are all about helping people! Of course the people we like to help the most are ourselves!
I'm Chunky! People think Slick and his son Big Loss keep me around for comic relief, but that's not true. I'm actually very smart! How smart? I have a team of writers on this show coming up with my "dumb" lines! God, I love reality TV!
WRITER: DICK DEBARTOLO ARTIST: TOM BUNK
Here's how the show works: I come back here to my office where the customer can't hear me and I tell the TV audience how much I really want to buy an item someone's brought in and how much I'm willing to pay.
Meanwhile, outside the shop, the customer tells the TV audience how much they'd like to get for the item they brought in and what's the lowest amount of money they'll take.
There's just one difference! The customer can't hear what I'm prepared to pay, but the producers secretly tell me what the lowest amount of money the customer is willing to take!
That's why the odds of us making money here in the pawn shop are 100 times better than the money the slots make for the casinos!
Original Rembrandt
SEARCH
HISTORY
AWN
TARS
LAS
OPEN 24 HRS
CASINO
flamingo
PAWN SHOP
MOTEL
BLA BLA
I ♥ MAD

I have something amazing to sell! This flintlock was owned by Davy Crockett!
What proof do you have that it was actually owned by Davy Crockett?
See the initials engraved on the handle? DC!
The handle says CD, not DC!
Er...er... yeah, CD stands for Crockett, Davy! That's how they did it the old days!
SALE
CD
If this really is Davy Crockett's flintlock, it would date back to 1822! James Graham would have most likely crafted it and today it would be worth a fortune! Crockett loved his gun so much he affectionately named it "Old Betsy," after his wife or his sister!
Your father sure knows a lot about history!
Actually, he knows nothing about history bu a lot about Google! That' another reason he runs back to his office so much So he can do a quick web search and then pretend he's some kind of genius
CRAP
A-Z
LAMPS
HISTORY
ANTIQ
SELL EXPENSIVE
A-Z
B-S
GUNS
BUY CHEAP
HOW TO CHEAT
I'm not convinced this flintlock is authentic! Is it okay if I call in an expert?
I'd prefer to call in an expert of my own?
Sure, no problem! You can call in an expert from this list of two that are on our payroll! I'd call the one who lives in Vegas. The other one lives in Rome, Italy and he'd have to come here at your expense. But the choice is yours!
MADE IN HONG KONG
SALE
I'm here with John Slanina, an expert on firearms! So John, what's your expert opinion about this?
If this really is Davy Crockett's flintlock, it would date back to 1822! James Graham would have most likely crafted it and today it would be worth a fortune! Crockett loved his gun so much he affectionately named it "Old Betsy," after his wife or his sister!
*&^% John, if you're going to Google the exact same information I Google, I'll get myself a new expert!
OLD BETSY
So what do you think this rifle's worth, John?
According to the phone message you left me earlier, I'd say it's worth between $40 and $45!
Are you kidding me? This is a one-of-a-kind historical artifact in perfect condition!
Perfect condition?? The stock is cracked, the barrel is rusty...
Okay, you've got a point! Give me a minute. I have another one in my car!
WANTED
HOTE
CASINO
CIGARETTE LIGHTER DE LUXE
ZZZ

This is the original envelope Abraham Lincoln used when he wrote the Gettysburg Address! See, it's right there on the back!
Well, now I know you're lying!
What makes you say I'm lying?
Because any idiot knows the address goes on the front of the envelope!
Linkoln Adress

This isn't that kind of address. This is the original, famous Lincoln's Gettysburg Address!
Wow, I get it now! Can I hold it?
Okay, but don't smear the ink! It's not dry yet. Ink from a fountain pen takes a long time to dry!
Sorry, pal, I still need proof this is real! See if you can get me Lincoln's cell phone number so I can give him a call and ask him about it. Then come back and we'll talk. I'm not stupid, you know!
Linkoln Adress

What's the most important thing Slick considers before making an offer?
A. How good it looks on camera.
B. How much he can B.S. about the item.
C. How likely Chunky is to make a stupid comment about it?
Answer:
D: How stupid Chunky will look playing with it on camera.
DUMB DUMBER & CHUNKY

This is Sick Restorations. When we buy collectables that are in sad shape we bring them here. Sick is the master at making the old new again! Just yesterday we brought Sick a rusted out 1907 Harley Davidson Motorcycle!
It was a total disaster, but we only paid $50 for it!
That was thanks to me you paid $50! The guy was looking for between $35 and $40. I was the one who talked him up to $50. Wait a minute — I think I screwed up again! Darn!

This is it! The entire frame was rusty, so I replaced it. The engine was frozen, so I put in a bigger, better one. The instruments on the dash were beyond repair, so I replaced them. New gas tank, new lights, new upholstery!
My God, this is your best job ever! It looks brand new! What'd you spend?
Probably more than you wanted, $18,000.
$18,000! I could have bought a brand new Harley for that amount!
Actually, I'll tell you the truth. That's exactly what I did! No one could save that hunk of crap you brought in!
Look at the bright side — we only lost $50 on the deal!
OIL

What the *&^% happened here??
This dude brought in this Civil War cannon to sell and I didn't want to make an offer until I knew if it still fired! That was your advice, grandpa!
A bit more advice — always take a *&^%ing cannon outdoors before you check if it still fires!
I'll have him fire it again, and we will be outdoors!
The only way I'd let you fire it again is if you'd promise to stand in front of it!
CASINO
OFFICE
Whaddya got and how much do you want?
I have 3 large pizzas and 2 six packs of beer in an insulated bag. I'm looking for $40!
I'll give you $32!
I'm not a customer!! This is the food Chunky ordered! It's $40!
Sorry, but I have to make some money on every transaction here. Here's $34. I'll get $40 from Chunky. 20% for me isn't too bad for the time I spent. Now get out!

I was sent over here to sign the paperwork on this birdcage. I can't believe the old man offered me $200!
Yes, he offered $200, but you'll really get $100! $200 was the OCO!
OCO? What's the OCO?
That's the On-Camera-Offer! The owners want to look generous and like they're not out to rip people off when the camera's running, but once it's off, it's SY — Screw You!

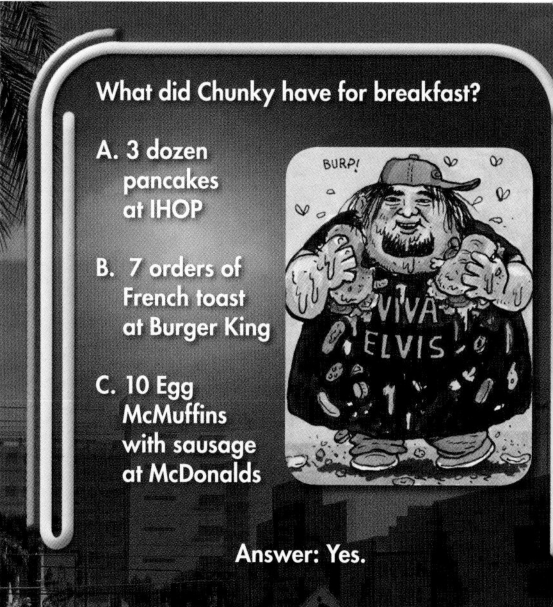
What did Chunky have for breakfast?
A. 3 dozen pancakes at IHOP
B. 7 orders of French toast at Burger King
C. 10 Egg McMuffins with sausage at McDonalds
BURP!
VIVA ELVIS
Answer: Yes.

You guys always put me down, but today you're going to be proud of me! I bought this for $2,500!
Wow! That's an original Airstream Camper! Airstream is like the premiere builder of luxury recreational vehicles in the U.S.! Fixed up, that baby could go for as much as $30,000!
Chunky, for the first time since you started working here, you made a good deal! Is the camper in the parking lot? I'm dying to see it in person!
Camper? What camper? I bought this picture of the Airstream for $2,500! The guy swore it's the only picture of that trailer!
Do me a favor, go stand in front of the cannon!

JOKE AND DAGGER DEPT.

SPY VS SPY VS SPY

WRITER AND ARTIST: ANTONIO PROHIAS   COLORIST: CARRIE STRACHAN

PHASING REALITY DEPT.

It is widely believed that a person experiences four psychological phases when grieving over death. They are: Denial—you refuse to believe the obvious; Anger—you get really pissed off at the circumstances; Depression—you become distressed at the realization; Acceptance—okay, you just deal with it. Here at MAD, we figured that there are some other situations in life when people experience these same grieving phases! So, we will now ask you to look at yourself and your emotions as you read up on...

BEING FAT

DENIAL

ANGER

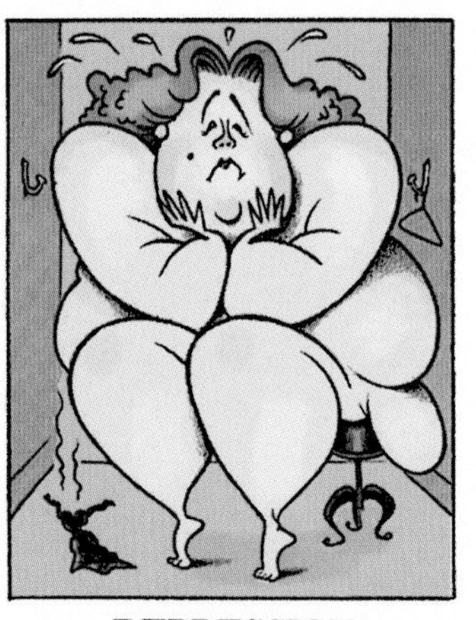

DEPRESSION

ACCEPTANCE

AGING

DENIAL

ANGER

DEPRESSION

ACCEPTANCE

BEING LOST

DENIAL

ANGER

DEPRESSION

ACCEPTANCE

MAD STAGES OF...

WRITER AND ARTIST: RICK TULKA
COLORIST: CARL PETERSON

BALDNESS

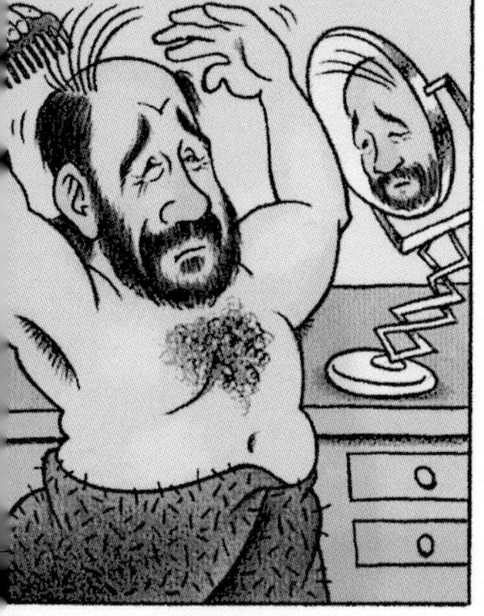

DENIAL

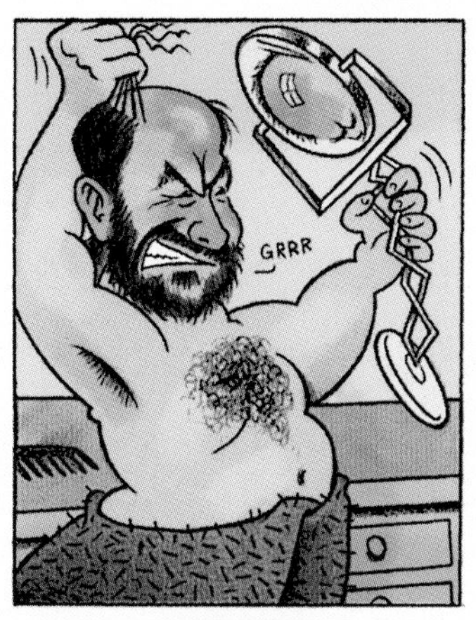

ANGER

DEPRESSION

ACCEPTANCE

NAUSEA

DENIAL

ANGER

DEPRESSION

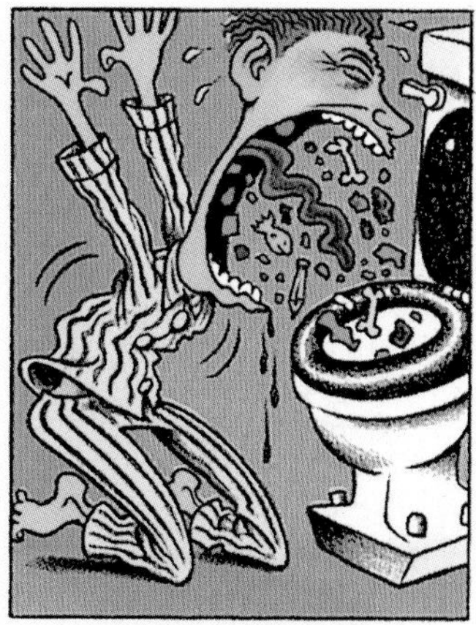

ACCEPTANCE

STUPIDITY

DENIAL

ANGER

DEPRESSION

ACCEPTANCE

And now, because Al Jaffee needs money to pay for a new summer wardrobe, we present...

SNAPPY ANSWERS TO STUPID QUESTIONS

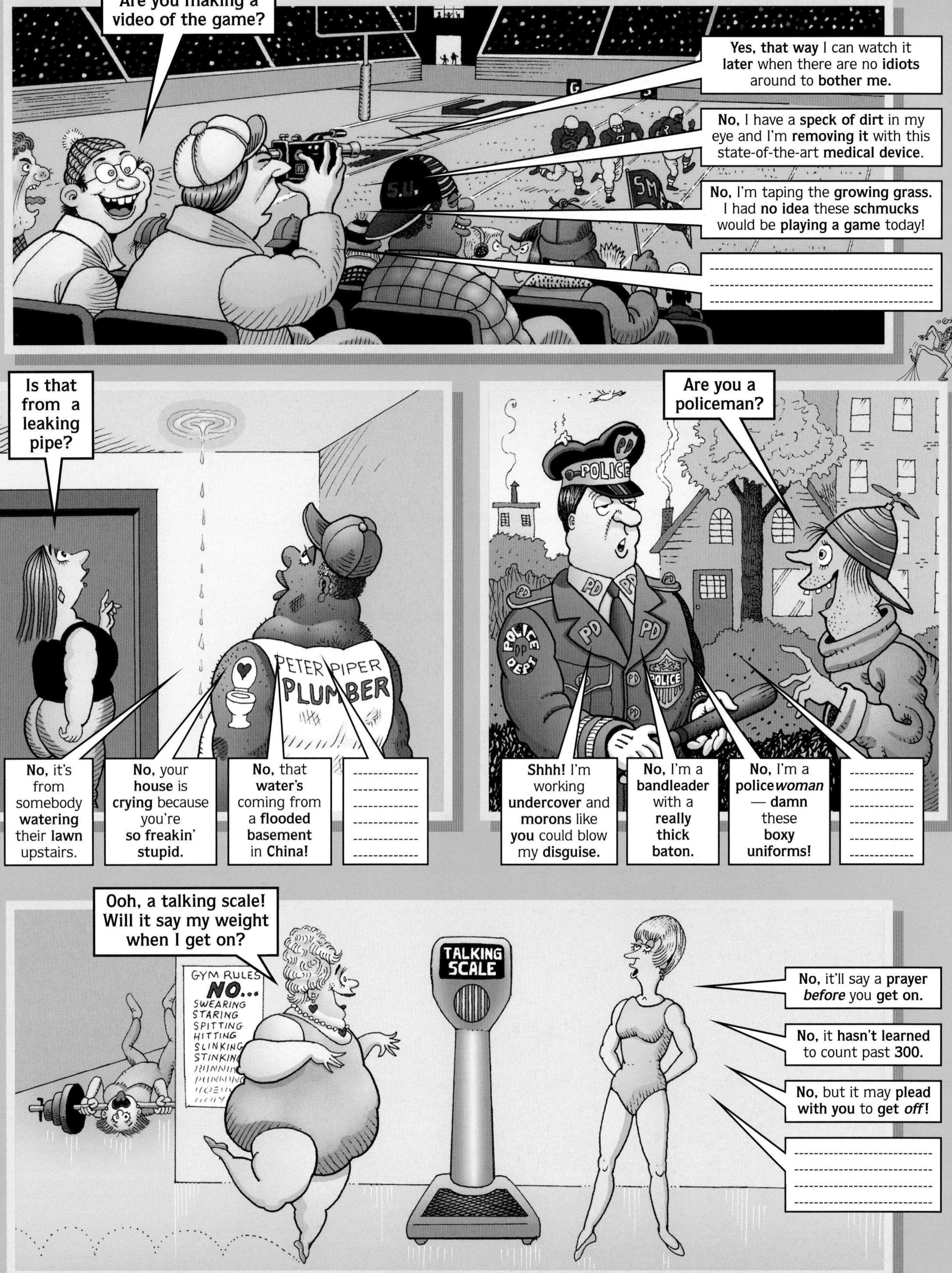

ARTIST AND WRITER: AL JAFFEE COLORIST: WILDSTORM

SNAPPY ANSWERS TO STUPID QUESTIONS

ONE AFTERNOON AT ROCKY'S DINER

WRITER AND ARTIST: DON MARTIN

The Internet is so wonderful! With its seemingly infinite number of sites, pages and links, you can get lost for hours searching and surfing the Web. But if you *really* want to get lost for hours, there's one website you have to visit...

MapMess: Home

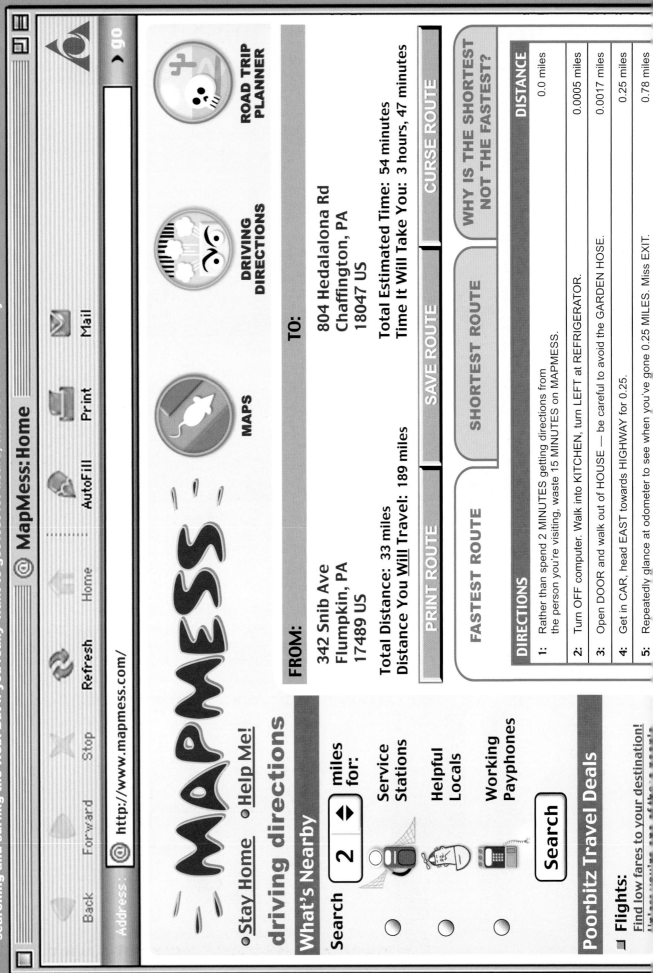

Back Forward Stop Refresh Home AutoFill Print Mail

Address: http://www.mapmess.com/ go

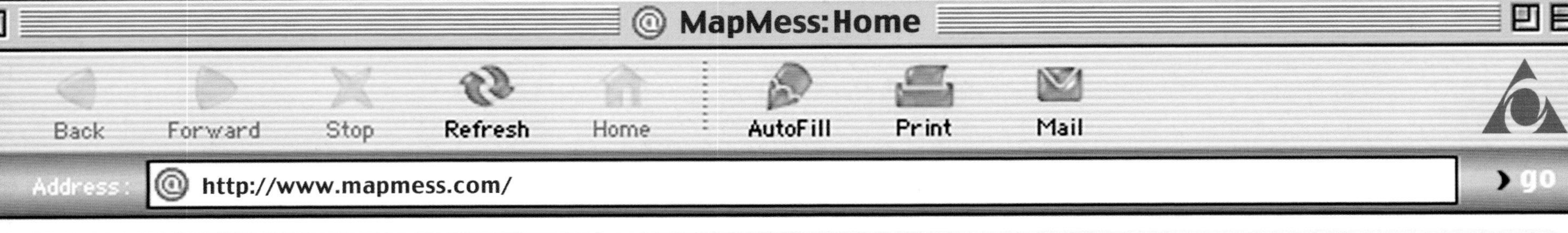

Stay Home   Help Me!

driving directions

What's Nearby

Search 2 miles for:

Service Stations

Helpful Locals

Working Payphones

Search

Poorbitz Travel Deals

- **Flights:**
  Find low fares to your destination!

FROM:	TO:
342 Snib Ave Flumpkin, PA 17489 US	804 Hedalalona Rd Chaffington, PA 18047 US
Total Distance: 33 miles Distance You Will Travel: 189 miles	Total Estimated Time: 54 minutes Time It Will Take You: 3 hours, 47 minutes

PRINT ROUTE | SAVE ROUTE | CURSE ROUTE

FASTEST ROUTE | SHORTEST ROUTE | WHY IS THE SHORTEST NOT THE FASTEST?

	DIRECTIONS	DISTANCE
1:	Rather than spend 2 MINUTES getting directions from the person you're visiting, waste 15 MINUTES on MAPMESS.	0.0 miles
2:	Turn OFF computer. Walk into KITCHEN, turn LEFT at REFRIGERATOR.	0.0005 miles
3:	Open DOOR and walk out of HOUSE — be careful to avoid the GARDEN HOSE.	0.0017 miles
4:	Get in CAR, head EAST towards HIGHWAY for 0.25.	0.25 miles
5:	Repeatedly glance at odometer to see when you've gone 0.25 MILES. Miss EXIT.	0.78 miles

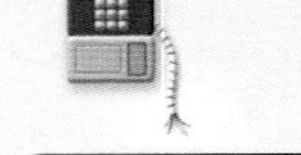

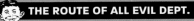

Rental Cars:

Find special offers on rental prices when our directions cause you to back over tire-shredding spikes in a commercial parking lot!

Lodging:

Save up to 70% on Poorbitz Savers when you're too ashamed to go home after failing to reach your destination!

Route Overview:

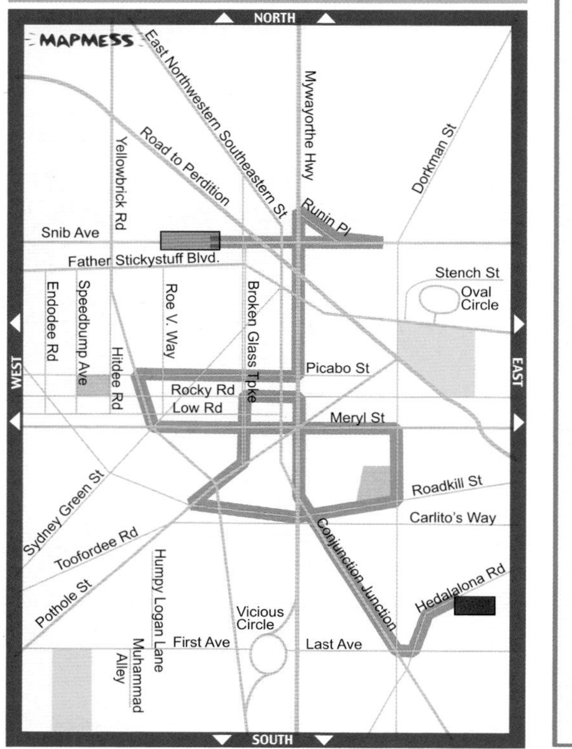

8:	Do not respond to passenger's muttered insult about relying on MAPMESS.	0.0 miles
9:	Ignoring uncomfortable silence that has settled over car, narrowly avoid a collision as you check directions while merging onto HIGHWAY (portions toll).	1.4 miles
10:	Frantically realize you're stuck in an "E-Z PASS" lane.	0.35 miles
11:	Spend a honking and profanity-filled 3 MINUTES tying up traffic, attempting to merge into "Cash/Tokens," 2 LANES over.	0.06 miles
12:	Once on HIGHWAY, note mild panic when you realize that MAPMESS failed to take into account the CONSTRUCTION that has closed EXIT 2 for the next 27 WEEKS.	1.7 miles
13:	Drive SEVERAL miles, using the inapplicable directions and your own navigational skills to devise a NEW route.	6.9 miles
14:	Notice that you're 30 MINUTES LATE and TOTALLY LOST.	14.7 miles
15:	Pull into gas station and show MAPMESS directions to old man sitting by the COKE MACHINE. Get back in car after geezer tells you, "I've lived around here for 63 years and I ain't never heard of none of these streets."	0.4 miles
16:	Consider stopping at PAY PHONE to CALL FRIEND for directions. Decide to KEEP DRIVING, rather than hear his sarcastic comments about your poor sense of direction.	15.3 miles
17:	Drive on for SEVERAL MORE MILES, try to convince yourself that you're driving "parallel" to the desired route.	7.4 miles
18:	Turn RIGHT, certain that you'll approach the desired route in a FEW MILES.	12.4 miles
19:	Give up after realizing that you've now been driving 1 HOUR and 45 MINUTES longer than MAPMESS's original estimated travel time.	27.9 miles
20:	Make another ILLEGAL U-TURN. Speed off, attempting to retrace your route and make up for lost time.	0.7 miles
21:	Immediately enter SPEED TRAP. MERGE RIGHT and enter SHOULDER as police car pulls you over and gives you another ticket.	0.02 miles
22:	Insane with frustration, do your best to stifle the urge to LUNGE for the OFFICER'S PISTOL.	0.0 miles
23:	As the OFFICER pulls AWAY, count backwards from TEN. Calm down enough to realize that you should have asked him for directions.	0.0 miles
24:	KEEP DRIVING, decide to recheck directions for any possible clues as to WHEREABOUTS.	9.8 miles
25:	While trying to retrieve the directions, which have fallen between the SEAT and the DOOR, crash into BARRIER.	.02 miles
26:	Call your AUTO CLUB. Have tow truck drop you off at 804 HEDALALONA ROAD.	47.2 miles

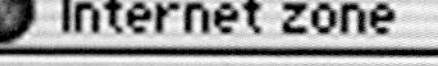
Internet zone

WRITER: JACOB LAMBERT

THE FOLKS ON YOU DEPT.

DON'T YOU HATE WHEN YOUR PARENTS...

If you're one of the lucky few who fully love, respect and admire your parents, we congratulate you on the tender, shining joy that is your life. But since you're probably *not* one of those pony-riding, bowtie-wearing mama's boys, we invite you to indulge your irritation by asking...

...refuse to buy you something because "you don't need it" – a rule which apparently doesn't cover *their* "necessities," like manicures, pedicures and *The Complete Fourth Season of Law & Order*?

...warn you not to "give in" to peer pressure – then burn with jealousy the minute your neighbors bring home a new Hummer?

...act as if you're a sullen jerk just because you don't feel like going into microscopic detail about every aspect of your horrible day?

...make you clean your room for "company" who won't come within fifty feet of it?

...ask you about kids you haven't talked to since preschool as if the two of you are still best buddies?

...offer to help with your homework when they clearly know even less than you do?

...invariably try to suck up all the credit when you do something well — and distance themselves from you as if you had the Asiatic Bird Flu when you screw up?

...make you do yard work on your only days off — so they can enjoy *theirs*?

WRITER: JACOB LAMBERT ARTIST: MARC HEMPEL

THE LONG-SUFFERING LACKEY'S LAMENT

WRITER AND ARTIST: DUCK EDWING

Sergio Aragonés Presents A MAD LOOK AT FISHING

WRITER AND ARTIST: SERGIO ARAGONÉS

SWAP MEET

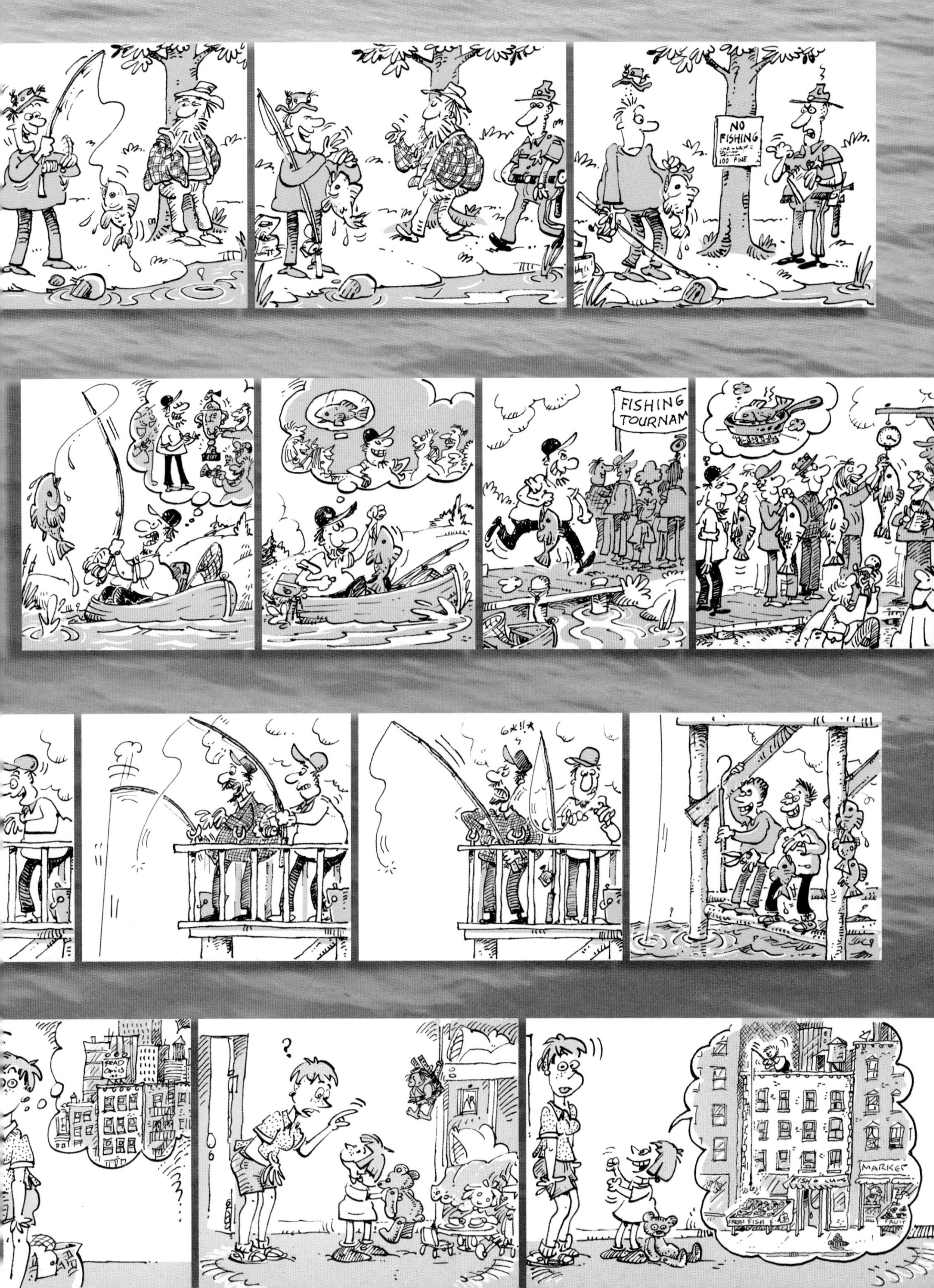
NO FISHING
100 FINE
FISHING TOURNAM
READ COMICS
FISH & CLAMS
MARKET
FRESH FISH
FRUIT

NUCLEAR WASTE
NUCLEAR WASTE
NO FISHING
NO FISHING
NO FISHING
NO FISHING
NO FISHING
ARAGONÉS

A LONG PHRASE JOURNEY INTO BLIGHT DEPT.

In a world where "image is everything," companies spend billions trying to come up with just the right slogan that concisely sums up what they're all about. But brevity comes at the cost of truthfulness, which is why you should probably check out these…

UNABRIDGED CORPORATE SLOGANS (PART II)

CNN The Most Trusted Name In News

…at least compared to those dweebs at FOX!

Do what tastes right, right up until the quadruple bypass surgery!

PBS Be More boring than you'd ever thought possible!

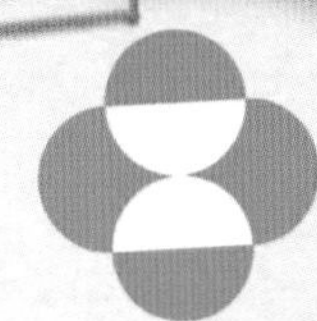

MERCK

Where patients come first to let us know that they're suing our butt!

at&t Your World. Delivered.

…But barely audible over the static!

you can get it on ebay

–then get rid of the same trash on eBay a month later!

McDonald's

I'm Lovin' it, except for the violent acid reflux at 2 AM!

tbs very funny

…is probably not the best description for endless reruns of "Becker" and "Home Improvement"!

My life. AMERICAN EXPRESS My card.

My God, look at this bill!

WRITER: JACOB LAMBERT

WHY DON'T YOU GO TO HEALTH? DEPT.

Only an absolute moron would go to a fast food place to eat healthy. Yet, there's always some stupid report telling you what the most "health-conscious" option on the menu is, and warning you about the worst. Here's a hint — it's ALL terrible for you! Still, we feel duty-bound to present:

The FDA'S Guide to the BEST &

	BEST	WORST
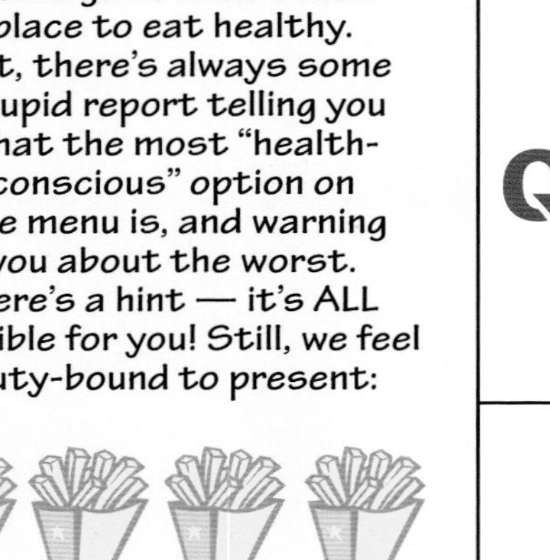	1" Lettuce Sub w/o mayo (15 calories)	8-Foot Beef Tallow-Parmesan Personal Party Sub (50,600 calories)
	Cajun-Steamed Imitation Anchovy Filet (75 calories)	 Deep Fried Whale Flank n' Fries Meal (12,400 calories)
	Breadless Pita & Tomato Wrap (10 calories)	 All-You-Can-Eat Salami Trough (calories vary)
	 Small Chili, Without Human Appendages (345 calories)	 Quintuple Breakfast Croissant Thingy (10,003 calories)

WORST CHOICES *in* FAST FOOD

WRITER:
JEFF KRUSE

PHOTOGRAPHER:
IRVING SCHILD

Nothing
(0 calories)

... & Bacon-Filled-Crust Pizza with Extra Cheese-Filled Pepperoni (83,000 calories)

Sticker of Christina Aguilera from Vending Machine by Entrance (50 calories)

Grande Belchorito con Mucho Queso (7,950 calories)

Cup of McWater, no McIce (185 calories)

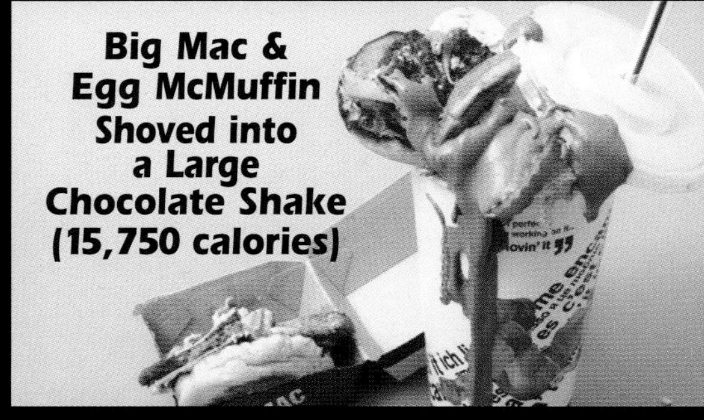

Big Mac & Egg McMuffin Shoved into a Large Chocolate Shake (15,750 calories)

Wet Napkin (3 calories)

Triple-Bacon Cheeseburger Smuggled in From Burger King (calories too high to count)

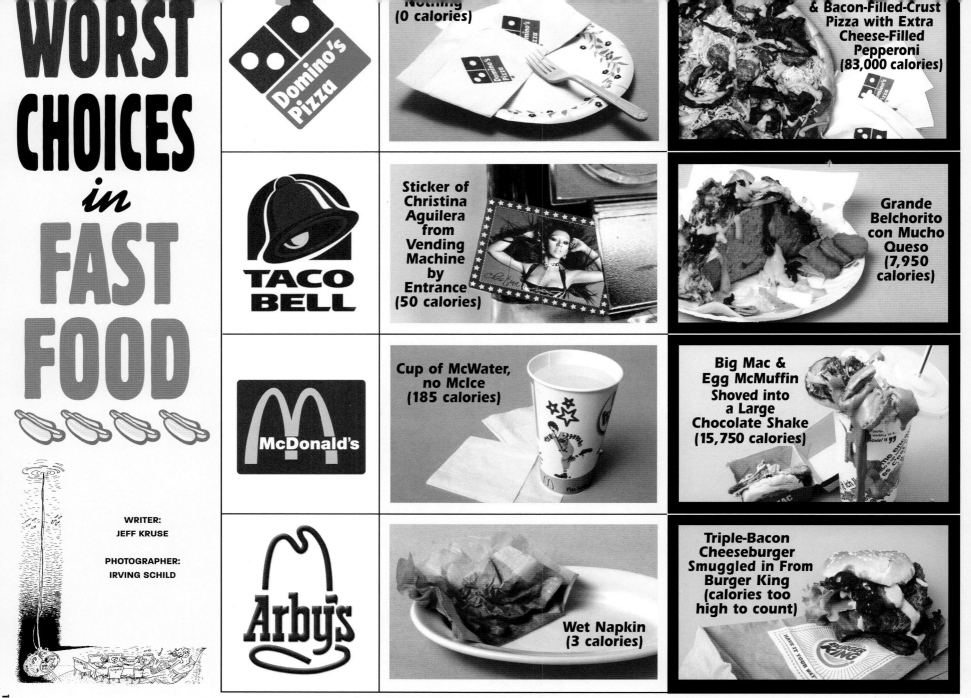

Robots are slowly taking over the jobs that humans used to do — from building cars to hosting TRL (unless we're wrong about Vanessa Minnillo...). And it's only a matter of time before these freakin' androids are working in our homes, too! And then what happens? Uh...actually, we're not sure... Man, we could really use a robot to finish this stupid intro for us! While we go back to the lab, why don't you read...

JOHN CALDWELL'S

YOU'VE DEFINITELY BOUGHT THE WRONG ROBOT IF...

...you've owned it less than a week and have already worn out three Allen wrenches.

...it's one of those older models, easily taken in by clever telemarketing scams.

...its only high-tech, labor-saving feature is a built-in pencil sharpener.

...in a matter of a few short days it's managed to turn the rest of your appliances against you.

WRITER AND ARTIST: JOHN CALDWELL

...it shorts out and smokes like a babyback rib on even the lowest *Jeopardy!* category.

...it's hogging all the three-way adaptors.

...it's constantly bringing home stray Roombas.

...it's up to a fifty dollar a day WD-40 habit.

...in the owner's manual under "troubleshooting" the lone entry reads "under no circumstances should you try to shoot back."

Subscribe to MAD!
You'll Never Miss An Issue... and Neither Will Your Bird!
6 Issues for only $19.99
(Cheep! Cheep! Cheep!)
Flock to www.madmag.com
or call 1-800-4 MAD MAG
6 2 3 6 2 4
Mon-Fri 6 a.m.-8 p.m. Sat 7 a.m.-4 p.m. Sun 8 a.m.-4 p.m. Eastern Time
$19.99 offer valid for U.S. and Canada orders only! Foreign orders please add $10.
If under 18, please be sure to get your parrot's permission!